The Power of AI Mom

A Beginner's Guide to Utilising AI for Productive Parenting

Jess W

Fitmumhub

Introduction

Welcome to "The Power of AI Mom," a book crafted specifically for full-time mothers curious about the world of Artificial Intelligence (AI) and its practical applications in everyday life.

Many of us mothers have harboured the dream of writing our book, a dream that, more often than not, remains just that - a dream. Caught up in the whirlwind of parenting and daily responsibilities, this aspiration frequently lingers in the background, unfulfilled yet persistent.

Yet, in this age of technological advancement, Artificial Intelligence (AI) can help us turn our dreams into reality. For mothers aiming to self-publish, AI offers invaluable resources. It can assist in designing covers, formatting pages, and even marketing the finished book by analysing market trends and identifying the target audience.

AI is a supportive partner in the writing journey, handling the heavy lifting in various aspects of book creation. This allows you, as a mother and a writer, to focus more on the creative aspects of your story, bringing your unique perspective and voice to life. With AI by your side, the dream of writing and publishing your book is no longer just a distant aspiration but a tangible, achievable goal.

If I can embark on this journey of writing a book, so can you. We often underestimate our capabilities, but with determination, passion, and the right tools, such as AI, achieving the goal of writing a book is within reach for all of us. Every mother has unique experiences and insights that can translate into compelling stories or valuable guidance. AI supports and simplifies the process, making what once seemed an overwhelming task entirely manageable.

Remember, writing a book isn't just about stringing words together; it's about sharing your perspective, learning, and journey, something every mother is richly equipped with. AI is here to help bridge the gap between your invaluable experiences and a finished, published book that reflects them. So, if you've ever dreamed of writing a book, now is the perfect moment to begin.

If you've ever felt overwhelmed by the rapidly evolving digital world or wondered how technologies like ChatGPT and AI can fit into your busy life as a mother, this book is for you. As a full-time mom, I understand the constant juggling between managing a household, nurturing children, and finding time for personal growth. Our days are often a whirlwind of activities, from the early morning school runs to bedtime stories, with endless chores and decisions in between. In this fast-paced life, wouldn't it be wonderful to have a helping hand – one that's informed by intelligent technology?

This book aims to bridge the gap between the complex world of AI and the everyday tasks and challenges you face as a mother. AI is no longer just a buzzword or a concept in sci-fi movies; it's a reality, enhancing lives in countless ways. From organising schedules to aiding in your child's education, from helping you start a home-based business to managing your mental health, AI can transform your daily routines into more manageable, efficient, and enjoyable experiences.

"The Power of AI Mom" is designed to be your companion in simplifying the concepts of AI. You don't need a background in technology to understand its contents. Instead, you'll find simple explanations, practical tips, and relatable examples showing how AI and tools like ChatGPT can seamlessly integrate into motherhood.

I will start with the basics, introducing you to what AI and ChatGPT are, and gradually explore various applications in areas crucial to you – as a parent, a home manager, and an individual with unique needs and aspirations. Whether through smart home devices that ease daily chores, AI-driven fitness apps that cater to your health, educational tools that support your children's learning, or AI-guided strategies to kickstart a business venture, this book covers a spectrum of possibilities AI brings to your doorstep.

As we embark on this journey together, remember that embracing AI is not about replacing the human touch with technology. It's about leveraging these tools to enhance your capabilities, giving you more time and space to focus on what truly matters – your family, your passions, and your well-being.

So, let's dive in and explore how you, as a full-time mom, can become an AI Mom – confident, informed, and ready to make the most of what AI offers in parenting.

Welcome to your journey into the world of AI, tailored for the superhero in every mother.

Your Guide [Jess]

Understanding AI and Its Potential

At its core, AI is about creating intelligent machines that can think, learn, and make decisions that mimic human intelligence. AI is becoming integral to our daily lives, from voice-activated assistants like Alexa and Siri to more complex systems that can diagnose diseases or predict weather patterns.

For mothers, this technology is not just about sophisticated gadgets but practical solutions. Imagine a world where your fridge can remind you to buy milk, an app can suggest the perfect nutrition plan for your family, or a virtual tutor can provide personalised learning experiences for your children. That's the world AI is building for us.

The Purpose of This Book

This book aims to demystify AI and show you, step by step, how it can be seamlessly integrated into your life. You'll discover how AI can help manage your home more efficiently, support your children's education, maintain your family's health and well-being, and even pursue your passions and career goals.

More importantly, this book is about empowerment. It's about taking charge of these technological tools and using them to create more time, space, and energy for the things that matter most to you. Whether starting a home-based business, learning a new skill, or simply finding more time to relax and enjoy your family, AI can be the bridge that takes you there.

Welcome to the Future: Embracing AI in Motherhood

In today's fast-paced world, where technology touches every aspect of our lives, Artificial Intelligence (AI) has emerged as a groundbreaking force, reshaping how we live, work, and interact. For full-time mothers, the advent of AI brings unique opportunities and challenges. This book is dedicated to you: the unsung heroes, the nurturers, the multi-taskers, and the chief decision-makers of your households. It's about how AI can simplify your day-to-day tasks and empower you to achieve, learn, and be more.

As a full-time mother myself, juggling parenting responsibilities and personal aspirations, I understand the delicate balance of managing a household while pursuing personal interests and goals. AI technology, often perceived as a tool for businesses and tech enthusiasts, is, in fact, a powerful ally for mothers everywhere. It can offer you new ways to manage your time, enhance your family's health and education, and even kickstart your journey towards financial independence.

Join the Journey

As we embark on this journey together, remember that the goal is not to become a tech expert overnight. Instead, it's about understanding and utilising AI as a valuable resource in your life as a mother. This book is filled with practical advice, real-life examples, and straightforward explanations to guide you every step of the way.

So, let's begin this exciting journey of exploration and discovery. Together, we'll unlock the potential of AI to transform your life as a full-time mother, opening doors to new possibilities and opportunities.

Copyright Page

Chapter 1: The Basics of AI and ChatGPT

Demystifying Artificial Intelligence

Artificial Intelligence (AI) is a technology transforming our lives in countless ways. As full-time mothers, it's essential to understand this revolution, not just for our benefit but also for our families. In this chapter, we will demystify AI, breaking down its complexities into simple, understandable concepts.

1.1 What is Artificial Intelligence?

Artificial Intelligence (AI) is a branch of computer science focused on creating machines capable of performing tasks that typically require human intelligence. This includes learning, problem-solving, recognising patterns, understanding language, and making decisions. AI systems are designed to process large amounts of data, learn from this data, and then apply this learning to complete specific tasks and solve problems. Critical aspects of AI include:

Learning Processes: This involves acquiring information and the rules for using the information.

Reasoning Processes: Using the rules to reach approximate or definite conclusions.

Self-correction: Improving algorithms over time to make more accurate predictions or decisions.

AI is primarily divided into two categories:

Narrow AI: Also known as Weak AI, this type of AI operates within a limited context and is a simulation of human intelligence. Narrow AI is often focused on performing a single task extremely well, and while these machines may seem intelligent, they operate under a limited set of constraints and limitations. Examples include voice assistants like Siri and Alexa and recommendation systems like those on Netflix or Amazon.

General AI: Also known as Strong AI, this type of AI would have general intelligence comparable to human intelligence, meaning it can reason, solve problems, learn, plan, and communicate in any language. General AI is still theoretical and not yet realised in practice.

AI is used in various fields, from simple tasks like filtering spam emails to more complex ones like autonomous driving, medical diagnosis, and financial market analysis. The technology behind AI includes algorithms, neural networks, machine learning, and deep learning, all of which enable machines to process and learn from data, improving their performance over time.

In essence, AI represents a frontier in computing and technology where machines not only perform tasks that typically require human intelligence but also have the potential to transform industries and our everyday lives by automating processes and offering insights and efficiencies beyond human capabilities.

1.2 What is ChatGPT?

GPT stands for "Generative Pre-trained Transformer." This name encapsulates three key aspects of the technology:

1. Generative: This refers to the model's ability to generate text. It can create coherent and contextually relevant text based on the input it receives.

2. Pre-trained: The model has been trained on a vast dataset before it is fine-tuned for specific tasks. This pre-training allows the model to understand and generate human-like text.

3. Transformer: This is the type of neural network architecture used by GPT. The Transformer architecture is particularly effective for handling sequences of data, like sentences, and is known for its ability to manage long-range dependencies in text.

Overall, GPT models are designed to generate human-like text by predicting the next word in a sentence given all the previous words, and they are used in a variety of applications, including conversation AI, content creation, translation, and more.

ChatGPT is an example of an AI model designed to understand and generate human-like text, making it a practical implementation of AI technologies. The latest version of ChatGPT that was released is ChatGPT-4.

Welcome to the World of ChatGPT!

Imagine if you had a friend who was a bit like a superhero – someone who could answer almost any question you throw at them, come up with stories that whisk you away to magical lands, help you with your homework, and even teach you how to bake the yummiest chocolate cake. Sounds pretty amazing, right? Well, guess what? Such a friend exists, not a person, but a super-smart computer program called ChatGPT!

ChatGPT is like having a genie on your computer or phone – but instead of granting three wishes, it offers endless possibilities for learning, creating, and having fun. It's a bit like talking to a wise old owl, except this owl has read almost every book under the sun and can chat with you anytime, anywhere.

Now, you might wonder, "How can a computer program be so smart?" or "Is it really okay for my kids to chat with it?" Great questions! ChatGPT is a part of what grown-ups call Artificial Intelligence, or AI for short. This means it's designed to think and talk like a human, but it's still a machine at heart. It's been taught by some of the cleverest engineers to understand your questions and come up with helpful, informative, and sometimes downright hilarious responses.

In this guide, we're going to explore the magic behind ChatGPT. We'll learn how it works, discover all the cool things it can do for you, and share some tips on how you and your family can chat with it safely and have a blast doing so. From helping your kids ace their maths homework to settling debates about the fastest animal in the world (the peregrine falcon, by the way), ChatGPT is here to make your day brighter and more brilliant.

So, grab your explorer's hat and your curiosity because we're about to embark on an adventure into the world of AI with ChatGPT, your new friendly digital companion. Let's dive in and discover all the fun and learning that awaits!

What Exactly is ChatGPT?

Imagine you have a magic book. When you ask it a question, the pages flutter to the right spot and give you the answer. ChatGPT is like that book, but it's not magic; it's science! It's a computer program that can chat with you like texting a friend. The "GPT" in ChatGPT stands for "Generative Pre-trained Transformer," but don't worry, you don't need to remember that. Just think of it as a Genius Pal for Talking!

ChatGPT 3.5 ⌄

How can I help you today?

Write a thank-you note
to your babysitter for the last-minute help

Suggest some names
for my cafe-by-day, bar-by-night business

Write a SQL query
that adds a "status" column to an "orders" table

Write a text message
asking a friend to be my plus-one at a wedding

Message ChatGPT...

ChatGPT can make mistakes. Consider checking important information.

How Does ChatGPT Work?

ChatGPT works by using something called artificial intelligence, or AI. This AI has read many books, websites, and more to learn as much as possible. When you ask a question, it uses what it's known to give you the best answer. It's like having a friend with a super-powered brain who's read every book in the library – twice!

What Can ChatGPT Do for You?

By now, you've met ChatGPT, your new AI buddy. This section is like opening a treasure chest filled with the most incredible, fun, and beneficial things ChatGPT can do for you and your family. Let's dive in and discover the gems waiting inside!

Homework Helper Extraordinaire

Kids, have you ever been stuck on a homework question, wishing for a helper to appear? Moms, have you ever found yourselves googling to help with school projects late at night? ChatGPT to the rescue! Whether maths puzzles, science facts, or history timelines, ChatGPT can explain and simplify complex ideas and guide you through learning new concepts. It's like having a tutor available 24/7, right at your fingertips!

Master Storyteller

Imagine a storyteller who can whisk you away to any world you wish. Do you want to hear about dragons, explore outer space, or dive underwater? ChatGPT can create stories for you with heroes, adventures, and magical lands. It's a fantastic way to spark creativity, inspire your storytelling, and enjoy new bedtime tales every night.

The Learning Buddy

Curiosity is the key to learning, and there's no question too big or small for ChatGPT. Wondering why the sky is blue, how aeroplanes stay up, or who invented ice cream? Just ask! ChatGPT can help you discover fun facts and explore the world's wonders. It's like going on a global adventure from the comfort of your home.

Your Creative Coach

Need inspiration for your next art project or ideas to write your poem? ChatGPT can spark your imagination with creative prompts, suggest art projects, and even help you overcome writer's block. It's like having an art teacher and a writing coach continuously ready to inspire your next masterpiece.

Fun and Games Friend

Looking for new games to play or fun activities to do? ChatGPT can create exciting games, riddles, and puzzles for the whole family to enjoy. It's a great way to have fun, challenge your brains, and enjoy quality family time.

Your Personal Assistant

Moms, imagine having a personal assistant to help you plan meals, organise your day, or brainstorm gift ideas. ChatGPT can offer suggestions for healthy recipes, remind you of important tasks, and even help you plan the perfect birthday party. It's like having an extra pair of hands to help you manage the busy life of a super mom.

Staying Safe and Smart

Remember to chat smartly and safely as we explore all the fun and helpful things ChatGPT can do. Always keep personal information private, and use this AI tool to enhance learning and creativity, not replace it.

Let's Get Chatting!

Armed with knowledge and ready for adventure, it's time to start chatting with ChatGPT. What will you discover first? A new story, a fun fact, or a creative project? There are endless possibilities, and ChatGPT is here to explore them all with you.

Creative Projects with ChatGPT

After exploring what ChatGPT can do, it's time to roll up our sleeves and dive into some creative projects. ChatGPT isn't just about answering questions or doing homework; it's a launchpad for imagination, creativity, and fun! Let's discover how you can use ChatGPT to bring your creative ideas to life, embark on learning adventures, and create memorable family moments.

Crafting Your Own Stories

Stories are windows to new worlds; with ChatGPT, you can be the architect of your adventures. Here's how to craft a tale together:

- Start with an Idea: Pick a setting, character, or theme. Maybe a pirate adventure, a journey through space, or a day in the life of a talking cat.

- Ask for a Storyline: Use ChatGPT to help build a storyline. Ask it to suggest plot twists, character names, and exciting events.

- Write Together: Take turns writing paragraphs with ChatGPT. You write one, then ask ChatGPT to write the next. Before you know it, you'll have a story co-authored by your family and AI!

Learning Through Quizzes

Quizzes are a fun way to learn new things. With ChatGPT, you can create custom quizzes on any topic you're curious about:

- Pick a Subject: Choose something you're learning in school or a fun topic, like dinosaurs, space, or famous inventors.

- Create Questions: Ask ChatGPT to come up with quiz questions. You can even challenge ChatGPT to make them tricky or include fun facts as hints.

- Quiz Time: Have a family quiz night where everyone guesses the answers. It's fun to learn together and see who the quiz champion is!

Art and Poetry Collaborations

Unleash your inner artist and poet with ChatGPT as your muse:

- Poetry Creation: Choose a theme for your poem, like nature, friendship, or dreams. Ask ChatGPT for a first line and take turns adding lines to create your family poem.

- Art Project Ideas: Looking for your next art project? Ask ChatGPT for ideas based on themes, materials you have at home, or the skills you want to practise. Whether it's drawing, painting, or crafting, ChatGPT can spark your creativity.

Plan a Family Adventure

Let ChatGPT help you plan an exciting family adventure, whether it's a real trip or a virtual exploration:

- Destination Ideas: Ask ChatGPT for suggestions on places to visit based on your interests, such as historical sites, nature parks, or science museums.

- Activity Planning: Once you have a destination in mind, ChatGPT can suggest activities. From scavenger hunts to educational games, make your outing extra special.

- Learning on the Go: Use ChatGPT to discover exciting facts about your destination. It's a great way to turn any trip into a learning adventure.

Cooking with AI

Explore new recipes and cooking projects with ChatGPT:

- Recipe Suggestions: Ask ChatGPT for recipe ideas based on ingredients you have at home or dietary preferences.

- Cook-Off Challenges: Create a cooking challenge where each family member picks a recipe ChatGPT suggests. See who can make the tastiest dish!

- Learn Cooking Tips: Not sure how to knead dough or chop vegetables properly? ChatGPT can offer cooking tips and tricks to improve your culinary skills.

With these project ideas, you're all set to use ChatGPT in fun and creative ways. Whether you're writing stories, learning new facts, expressing your creativity, planning adventures, or cooking up a storm, ChatGPT is here to make every experience more prosperous and enjoyable.

Safety Reminder:

While diving into projects with ChatGPT, remember to keep personal information private and ensure a safe browsing environment for kids.

Chatting Safely with ChatGPT

As we dive into the digital world, we must chat smartly and stay safe. ChatGPT is a fantastic tool for learning, creativity, and fun, but just like any adventure, knowing the safety rules makes the journey even better. Here's how you and your family can enjoy chatting with ChatGPT while keeping safety at the forefront.

Understanding ChatGPT's Boundaries

First, ChatGPT is super intelligent but only knows some things, and it certainly doesn't know you personally. Remember:

- Personal Info is Private: Never share your personal information, like your full name, address, phone number, or school. ChatGPT doesn't need to know where you live to tell you an incredible story about dinosaurs or help with maths homework.

- ChatGPT is Neutral: It's programmed to be helpful and informative without forming personal opinions or relationships. If it ever seems to say something off, it's not intentional and can be reported for improvement.

Smart Chatting Tips

To make the most out of your interactions with ChatGPT, keep these tips in mind:

- Be Clear and Specific: The more specific your questions or requests are, the better ChatGPT can help you. If you're looking for information on a project, mention what you're strictly looking for.

- Use it as a Learning Tool: Ask ChatGPT to explain concepts, solve problems step by step, or give you practice questions. It's like having a study buddy whenever you need it.

- Keep Conversations Appropriate: ChatGPT is designed to avoid inappropriate content, but it's still essential to steer conversations positively. Always be respectful and kind, as you would when talking to a friend.

Setting Up a Safe Chat Environment

Moms, here's how you can ensure a safe chatting environment for your kids:

- Explore Together: Initially, spend time exploring ChatGPT with your kids. It's a great way to teach them how to use it safely and responsibly.

- Monitor Use: Keep an eye on your kids' interactions with ChatGPT. Encourage them to share their learnings and questions with you.

- Use Parental Controls: Use any available parental controls or settings to manage and monitor your child's online activities.

Encouraging Open Communication

- Talk About Digital Safety: Use your time with ChatGPT to discuss the importance of digital safety and privacy. Encourage kids to ask questions and express any concerns they might have.

- Share and Learn Together: Make sharing exciting facts or stories from ChatGPT a fun family activity. It encourages learning and helps you monitor the content being explored.

Remember:

Chatting with ChatGPT is meant to be an enjoyable and educational experience. Following these safety tips sets the stage for a positive and enriching interaction with AI, ensuring that learning remains fun, safe, and effective.

Ready for Safe Adventures?

Now that we've covered how to chat safely with ChatGPT, you're all set for countless learning, creativity, and exploration adventures. Remember, the digital world is vast and exciting, and when navigated safely opens up endless possibilities for discovery.

Learning and Growing with ChatGPT

Welcome to a World of Endless Learning!

Remember every question you ask, every story you dive into, and every problem you solve with ChatGPT is a step forward in your journey of learning and growth. ChatGPT isn't just a tool for answering questions; it's a gateway to a universe brimming with knowledge, creativity, and opportunities for personal development for moms and kids alike.

Embracing Curiosity with ChatGPT

Curiosity is the engine of achievement. Here's how ChatGPT can be your fuel:

- Ask Anything: Encourage your kids to ask ChatGPT about anything. From "Why is the sky blue?" to "How do aeroplanes fly?" every question is an opportunity to learn something new.

- Explore Subjects: Use ChatGPT to deepen your knowledge of subjects you're learning at school or to explore new interests. Whether science, history, literature, or art, ChatGPT can provide insights, explanations, and resources.

Building Skills Together

ChatGPT can help develop essential skills that are crucial for both academic success and personal growth:

- Critical Thinking: Challenge yourselves to think critically by discussing the answers ChatGPT provides. Analyse the information, ask follow-up questions, and explore different viewpoints.

- Creativity: Use ChatGPT prompts to spark creativity. Write stories, compose poems, or create art based on ideas generated through your conversations.

- Problem-Solving: Approach ChatGPT with real-life problems or puzzles. It's a safe space to brainstorm solutions, practice decision-making, and think logically.

Learning Beyond the Classroom

The learning journey with ChatGPT continues beyond academic topics. It extends to life skills and interests that enrich your lives:

- Daily Life Questions: Use ChatGPT to learn about managing time, organising your space, cooking recipes, or understanding health and fitness. It's like having a knowledgeable friend ready to help with everyday queries.

- Hobbies and Interests: Whether you're interested in gardening, space exploration, coding, or crafting, ChatGPT can help you delve deeper into your hobbies. Learn new techniques, find interesting facts, or get inspired to start a new project.

A Partner in Personal Growth

For moms, ChatGPT can be a partner in your personal growth journey:

- Self-Improvement: Explore topics on self-care, mindfulness, fitness, or professional development. ChatGPT can offer resources, tips, and motivation.

- Lifelong Learning: Continue your education by learning new skills, and languages, or exploring subjects you've always been curious about. ChatGPT can guide you through the learning process, making it enjoyable and fulfilling.

Safety and Respect Always

As you learn and grow with ChatGPT, remember the importance of safe and respectful interactions. Reinforce the idea that while ChatGPT is a powerful learning tool, using it responsibly is critical to a positive experience.

The Adventure Continues

As this section concludes, remember that learning and growing with ChatGPT is an ongoing adventure. There's always something new to discover, a skill to master, or a challenge to overcome. Embrace each day as an opportunity to learn something new together as a family.

Stay curious, stay inspired, and let ChatGPT guide you to a world of knowledge and creativity. The learning path is endless, and every step taken is a step toward a brighter, more informed future.

1.3 How Does AI Work?

AI, or Artificial Intelligence, works by teaching computers to do tasks that would typically require human intelligence. Here's a simple explanation of how it works:

Learning from Data: Just like humans learn from experience, AI learns from data. You give the AI system a lot of information (data), which it uses to learn patterns, relationships, or features in this data. For example, by showing an AI thousands of pictures of dogs, it learns what a dog looks like.

Algorithms: An algorithm in AI is like a recipe with step-by-step instructions on performing a task. These algorithms analyse the data, learn from it, and then make decisions or predictions based on what they have learned.

Machine Learning: This is a crucial part of AI. It's like teaching a computer to figure things out independently based on the data it receives. The computer uses algorithms to find patterns and make decisions. Think of it as a child learning to differentiate between fruits by looking at different characteristics like colour, shape, and size.

Neural Networks: Imagine our brain with its network of neurons; neural networks in AI are somewhat similar. They are a series of algorithms that mimic the human brain's structure and function, helping the computer recognise patterns and solve common problems in the fields of AI, like speech recognition or image classification.

Training and Testing: AI systems are trained using large datasets. This is like practising or studying. The more data the AI system is trained on, the better it becomes at making predictions or decisions. Then, it is tested with new data to see how well it performs.

Improvement Over Time: Many AI systems improve as they get more data. This is known as 'learning'. The more they 'experience', the better they become at their tasks. For example, an AI that recommends movies improves as it learns your preferences over time.

In summary, AI feeds a computer a lot of data to learn from. It uses specific algorithms to process this data, discover patterns, and then make decisions based on what it has learned. This process is similar to how humans know from experience and use that knowledge to make decisions.

1.4 AI in Everyday Life

Artificial Intelligence (AI) has woven itself into the fabric of our daily lives, often without us even realising it. From the moment we wake up to when we go to bed, AI influences many activities. Here's how AI features in everyday life:

Smartphones and Personal Assistants:

- AI powers virtual assistants like Siri, Google Assistant, and Alexa. These assistants use voice recognition to respond to commands, help you schedule appointments, provide weather updates, and even control smart home devices.

Social Media and Online Shopping:

- AI algorithms personalise your experience on platforms like Facebook, Instagram, and YouTube by analysing your interactions and suggesting content you might like.

- In online shopping, AI recommends products based on your browsing and purchase history.

Navigation and Transportation:

- GPS navigation apps like Google Maps use AI to analyse traffic data in real-time, suggesting the fastest routes to your destination.

- Ridesharing apps like Uber use AI for price surging, optimising routes, and matching you with drivers.

Home Automation:

- Smart home devices, like lights, security cameras and thermostats use AI to learn your preferences and automate tasks accordingly.

Banking and Finance:

- AI detects fraudulent activities in your bank transactions by recognising unusual patterns.

- Many investment apps use AI to give personalised financial advice and automate trading.

Health and Fitness:

- Wearable devices like smartwatches use AI to monitor your health, track fitness activities, and provide health insights.

- AI in healthcare apps assists in symptom checking and early diagnosis.

Entertainment:

- Streaming services like Spotify and Netflix use AI to analyse your watching and listening habits and recommend movies, TV shows, or music tailored to your tastes.

Customer Service:

- Chatbots on various websites provide instant customer service and support by answering frequently asked questions and assisting with issues.

Email:

- AI helps filter spam emails and categorise incoming mail into primary, social, and promotional tabs in services like Gmail.

Photography:

- Smartphones use AI in their cameras for features like facial recognition, scene detection, and enhancing photo quality.

AI is like a silent helper, making daily tasks more convenient, efficient, and personalised. As technology advances, AI's role in our lives is poised to become more prominent, revolutionising how we live, work, and interact.

1.5 The Impact of AI on Mothers

Artificial Intelligence (AI) significantly impacts the lives of mothers, offering tools and solutions that can simplify, enhance, and bring efficiency to various aspects of motherhood. Here's how AI is making a difference:

Streamlining Household Management:

- AI-powered smart home devices can automate daily chores, like adjusting thermostats, controlling lights, or managing security systems, easing the burden of household management.

- Appliances like AI-enabled washing machines or robotic vacuums can learn preferences and optimise their functions, saving time and effort.

Enhancing Childcare and Education:

- AI-driven educational apps provide personalised learning experiences for children, adapting to their learning pace and style, which can significantly help homeschool or supplement school education.

- For younger children, AI-powered toys and games can offer interactive and educational experiences that entertain while they teach.

Health and Nutrition Management:

- AI in fitness apps can tailor workout and nutrition plans for mothers, helping them maintain their health and wellness.

- For family health, AI can track and analyse symptoms, suggest dietary recommendations, and even remind mothers of vaccination schedules and doctor's appointments.

Mental Health Support:

- AI-driven meditation and mindfulness apps can support mental health, offering personalised stress relief and mental well-being exercises.

- Chatbots and online platforms can offer emotional support and basic counselling, helping mothers to manage stress and anxiety.

Personalised Learning and Skill Development:

- AI opens up opportunities for personal growth, with online courses and learning platforms offering flexible learning schedules that fit into a busy mother's life.

- AI tools can assist in language learning, acquiring new hobbies, or even professional upskilling.

Budgeting and Financial Management:

- AI-driven financial apps can help mothers manage household budgets, track expenses, and provide insights into spending patterns for better financial planning.

Social Connectivity and Networking:

- AI algorithms in social media platforms can help mothers connect with supportive communities and parenting groups and find local events or resources.

Time Management and Productivity:

- AI can assist in organising schedules, setting reminders for important family events, and helping prioritise tasks, thus enhancing daily productivity.

Access to Information and Assistance:

- Virtual assistants, powered by AI, can provide quick information, answer queries, and assist in tasks like online shopping or searching for recipes, making information access more accessible and more efficient.

Empowering Entrepreneurship:

- For mothers pursuing business ventures, AI tools offer insights for market research, and customer behaviour analysis and automate routine tasks, facilitating entrepreneurship and home-based businesses.

Safety and Security:

- AI-powered home security systems provide enhanced safety features like facial recognition and real-time alerts, ensuring the family's safety and giving mothers peace of mind.

Customised Entertainment and Leisure:

- AI in entertainment platforms like streaming services ensures that mothers can find content suited to their tastes quickly and easily, optimising their limited leisure time.

In conclusion, AI significantly impacts full-time mothers by providing practical solutions, educational support, personal development opportunities, and a means to balance the multifaceted demands of motherhood. It's not just about technology; it's about empowering mothers with tools that make life more manageable and enjoyable. As AI continues to evolve, its role in facilitating and enriching the lives of full-time mothers is likely to grow even further.

1.6 Embracing AI Without Fear

For many mothers, the rapid advancement of Artificial Intelligence (AI) can seem daunting. The key to embracing AI lies in understanding its benefits and learning how to use it as a tool to enhance daily life. Here's how mothers can approach AI without fear and with confidence:

1. Understanding AI

Start by learning the basics of AI. Knowledge demystifies technology and reduces fear. Understand that AI is designed to assist and augment human activities, not replace them.

Here are some straightforward ways to learn about AI:

Using Smartphones and Virtual Assistants:

- Many smartphones come equipped with AI-powered virtual assistants like Siri or Google Assistant. Experiment with these by asking questions, setting reminders, or getting directions. Notice how these assistants understand your voice and learn from your requests.

Exploring AI in Social Media:

- Observe how social media platforms like Facebook or Instagram use AI to suggest friends, personalise your news feed, or recommend ads based on your activity. This practical example shows how AI tailors experience to individual users.

Trying Out AI in Online Shopping:

- Notice how online stores recommend products. These suggestions are based on AI algorithms analysing your browsing and purchase history, demonstrating how AI can predict your preferences.

Using AI for Navigation:

- Apps like Google Maps use AI to analyse traffic data and suggest the best routes. Mothers can use these navigation apps to see how AI provides real-time, practical solutions.

Playing with Educational AI Apps for Kids:

- Explore educational apps that use AI to create personalised learning experiences for children. These apps adapt to a child's learning pace and style, providing a hands-on example of AI in education.

Reading Simple AI Articles and Watching Videos:

- Look for simple articles, blogs, or videos explaining AI. Websites like Wired, TechCrunch, or even children's science sites can have easy-to-understand content about AI.

Attending Local Workshops or Webinars:

- Participate in community workshops or online webinars focused on introducing AI to beginners.

AI in Home Devices:

- Explore their features if you have smart home devices like a Nest thermostat or a smart fridge. These devices use AI to learn your preferences and automate home management tasks.

Experimenting with Simple AI Tools Online:

- There are many online tools and games that demonstrate AI in a simple and interactive way. For example, AI experiments by Google (g.co/aiexperiments) offer fun, hands-on experiences with AI.

Joining Online Parenting and Tech Forums:

- Engage with online forums or parenting groups where AI technology is discussed. It's a great way to learn from others' experiences and get recommendations for beginner-friendly AI resources.

By starting with these everyday examples and resources, moms can gradually build their understanding of AI in a way that's practical, relatable, and less intimidating. As confidence grows, more advanced concepts and applications can be explored.

2. Seeing AI as an Ally

Seeing AI as an ally involves recognising its helpful applications in daily life, especially in tasks and responsibilities typical for mothers. Here are some simple, real-world examples where AI can be seen as a supportive tool:

Virtual Assistants for Daily Organisation:

- Use AI-powered virtual assistants like Siri, Alexa, or Google Assistant to set reminders for family appointments, create shopping lists, play educational content for children, or even control smart home devices. This helps in organising daily tasks more efficiently.

Personalised Learning Aids for Children:

- AI-driven educational apps and online platforms can adapt to a child's learning style, offering personalised educational experiences. This could range from interactive learning games to

AI tutors that help with homework, making AI a valuable ally in supporting children's education.

AI in Meal Planning and Recipes:

- Use AI-powered recipe apps or websites that suggest meal ideas based on your dietary preferences, ingredients at home, or how much time you have to cook. This makes meal planning a lot less stressful and more efficient.

Efficient Housekeeping with Smart Home Devices:

- Employ smart home devices like robot vacuum cleaners, which use AI to navigate and clean the house more efficiently, saving time for other activities. Smart thermostats learn your family's routine and adjust the home temperature automatically for comfort and energy savings.

Health and Fitness Tracking:

- Wearable fitness trackers use AI to analyse physical activity, monitor health metrics, and provide personalised fitness advice. This can be an excellent way for mothers to track their health and wellness.

AI for Budgeting and Finance Management:

- Financial management apps with AI can track expenses, categorise spending, and offer insights for budget optimisation, making it easier to manage household finances.

Online Shopping Assistance:

- AI algorithms on e-commerce platforms provide personalised shopping recommendations, making online shopping quicker and more tailored to individual needs.

Content Filtering for Child Safety Online:

- AI-driven tools can help filter out inappropriate content, ensuring children's safety while they explore the internet.

Social Media Management:

- For mothers who manage a blog or a small business, AI tools can optimise social media posts for better engagement and suggest the best times to post.

In these examples, AI acts as an assistant, helping streamline tasks, providing personalised support, and offering solutions to make daily motherhood responsibilities more manageable. This portrayal of AI demonstrates its role as a supportive ally rather than something to be apprehensive about.

3. Starting Small

Begin with simple AI tools and applications. Use familiar platforms like voice assistants, recommendation systems on streaming services, or basic smart home devices. This gradual approach helps build comfort and familiarity.

4. Prioritising Safety and Privacy

Educate yourself about the safety and privacy aspects of AI tools. Use secure passwords, understand privacy settings, and teach your family about digital safety. Knowing that you're in control of your data and privacy can alleviate concerns.

For mothers using AI daily, prioritising safety and privacy is crucial. Here are several ways to ensure that interactions with AI are secure and private:

- Strong Passwords and Authentication:

Use strong, unique passwords for all AI-enabled devices and accounts. Consider using a password manager. Enable two-factor authentication (2FA) where available to add an extra layer of security.

- Regular Software Updates:

Regularly updates the software of AI devices and apps.

- Understanding Privacy Settings:

Familiarise yourself with the privacy settings of AI tools and platforms. Adjust settings to limit data sharing or turn off features you're uncomfortable using, especially those involving personal data or your children's information.

- Secure Home Network:

Ensure your home Wi-Fi network is secure. Use a strong Wi-Fi password, change it periodically, and choose a Virtual Private Network (VPN) for an added layer of security. A VPN establishes a private, secure network over a public one.

- Educating Children about Online Safety:

Teach your children about online safety. Explain to them the importance of not sharing personal information online and the basics of digital footprint management.

- Reviewing Data Collection Policies:

Read and understand the terms of service and privacy policies of AI applications and devices. Be aware of what data is being collected and how it's used.

- Using Trusted AI Services and Devices:

Choose AI products and services from reputable companies known for prioritising user privacy and security.

- Monitoring and Limiting Voice Assistant Use:

Be cautious about what is spoken around voice assistants. Disable or mute these devices during private conversations and teach family members to do the same.

- Being Wary of Camera and Microphone Access:

For devices and apps requesting access to your camera and microphone, grant permission only if necessary and from trusted apps. Cover webcams when not in use.

- Being Cautious with Personal Information: Be mindful of the personal information shared with AI-driven devices and platforms. Avoid sharing sensitive data unless it's essential.

- Backup Data Regularly:

Regularly backup vital data from AI devices or applications. This ensures data safety in case of a security breach or technical failure.

- Staying Informed about AI and Privacy:

Stay updated on the latest developments in AI technology and privacy. This can help you make informed decisions about using AI tools and protecting your family's data.

By taking these precautions, mothers can leverage the benefits of AI while ensuring their family's safety and privacy in the digital world.

5. Exploring Parenting-Specific AI Applications

Look for AI applications specifically designed for parenting. From apps that track developmental milestones to educational tools that adapt to your child's learning style, these applications are tailored to assist motherhood.

6. Learning Through Communities

Join online forums, social media groups, or local community groups where you can learn from other moms who are using AI in their lives. Sharing experiences and tips can be beneficial.

7. Staying Informed

Keep up-to-date with the latest developments in AI. Understanding how AI is evolving can help you anticipate how it can benefit your life as a mother.

8. Embracing AI for Personal Growth

Use AI for your personal development. Whether it's learning a new skill through an AI-powered platform, using fitness apps for health, or AI tools for pursuing a hobby, see AI as a facilitator for growth and learning.

9. Involving the Family

Make AI a part of family discussions. Involve your partner and children in learning about and using AI tools. This can help dispel myths and create a family-friendly approach to technology.

10. Balancing Technology with Human Interaction

Remember that AI is a supplement, not a replacement for human interaction and activities. Balance tech usage with real-world experiences to maintain a healthy digital lifestyle for you and your family.

11. Seeing the Bigger Picture

Recognise that AI is not just about cutting-edge gadgets but about making life easier and more enjoyable. Whether it's having more time for your children or reducing the stress of household management, AI can contribute positively to your life as a mother.

12. Adopting a Positive Mindset

Approach AI with curiosity and an open mind. Instead of fearing the unknown, focus on the potential benefits and how it can enhance your role as a mother.

In conclusion, embracing AI without fear involves understanding, starting small, ensuring safety, and seeing AI as an ally in the journey of motherhood. By adopting this technology at your own pace and with a positive mindset, you can harness its potential to simplify tasks, gain new knowledge, and spend more quality time with your family. When approached with awareness and caution, AI can be a powerful tool in making the challenging yet rewarding journey of motherhood a bit easier.

Chapter 2: AI in Daily Life: A Mother's Ally

2.1. Integrating AI into Your Daily Routine

Having understood the basics of AI, let's explore how it can be practically applied in your daily life as a full-time mother. This chapter dives into various aspects of household management, children's education, and health, showcasing how AI can be a significant ally in these areas.

2.1.1. Household Management Made Easier

Here are several examples of how AI can be utilised:

- Smart Home Assistants: Devices like Amazon Echo or Google Home can help organise daily routines. You can set reminders for laundry, dishwashing, or trash removal tasks. They can also help maintain a shopping list, set timers for cooking, or remind you of upcoming appointments.

- AI-Powered Scheduling Apps: Various AI-driven apps can help with scheduling household tasks. These apps can learn your preferences and routines over time and suggest optimal schedules for cleaning, grocery shopping, and other household duties.

- Robot Vacuums: AI-enabled robot vacuums like Roomba can automate the cleaning process. They can be scheduled to clean at certain times and learn the layout of your home for more efficient cleaning. Google DeepMind recently introduced Mobile Aloha, a low-cost robot capable of completing complex tasks like cooking, cleaning, and more. A Gas-pumping robot has been developed by the Danish company Autofuel. It is a fully automated robotic refuelling system, no human interaction is needed at all. The future we have all been waiting for might be here sooner than expected.

- Family Coordination Tools: AI can assist in coordinating tasks among family members. Using AI algorithms, apps like Cozi can help coordinate and communicate everyone's schedules and activities, track grocery lists, manage to-do lists, plan for dinner, and keep the whole family on the same page.

- Meal Planning and Prep: AI-based meal planning apps can suggest meal plans based on dietary preferences, past meal choices, and even what's in your fridge. This helps in reducing food waste and simplifies grocery shopping. Some popular meal-planning apps include MyFitnessPal, Yummly, Mealime, Paprika Recipe Manager, Plan to Eat, Eat This Much, PlateJoy, Pepperplate, Prepear and Tasty.

- Budget Management: AI-driven budgeting tools like Mint or YNAB can track expenses, categorise spending, and provide insights on better managing household finances. Here are some of the most well-known and widely used budget management apps: PocketGuard, EveryDollar, GoodBudget, Wally, Honeydue and Quicken.

- Energy Management: Smart thermostats, using AI, can learn your family's routine and adjust heating and cooling for optimal comfort and efficiency, helping to manage utility bills more effectively. Here are several examples of apps that can assist in managing and optimising your home's energy consumption. These include Nest, Hive, Sense, EcoFactor, OhmConnect, Energy Cost Calculator and SolarEdge Monitoring.

- Laundry Assistance: Some modern washing machines equipped with AI can suggest the best wash cycles based on the fabric type, load size, and degree of soiling, making laundry tasks more efficient.

- Child Safety Monitoring: AI-powered cameras and monitors can provide real-time alerts about children's activities, ensuring their safety at home.

- Interactive Learning for Kids: AI-driven educational apps and tools can keep children engaged in learning activities, giving moms more time to focus on other tasks.

By integrating AI technologies into daily routines, moms can significantly reduce the time and effort spent on household management, leading to a more organised, efficient, and balanced home environment.

2.2. Supporting Children's Education and Development

AI has a profound impact on learning and development, offering personalised educational experiences:

Here are several examples of how AI can be effectively utilised in this area:

- Personalised Learning Platforms: AI-driven educational software can adapt to each child's learning pace and style. Tools like Khan Academy, Udemy and Coursera offer customised learning paths, adjusting difficulty levels and topics based on the child's progress and understanding.

- Interactive Educational Games: AI-powered games make learning more engaging and fun. These games can adapt to a child's abilities, providing challenges that are neither easy nor hard, keeping them motivated and enhancing learning.

- Language Learning Apps: AI-based apps like Duolingo offer children interactive and personalised language learning experiences. They adjust lessons based on the learner's progress and retention rate.

- Homework Assistance: AI tools like Socratic can help children with homework by providing explanations, step-by-step guides, and educational resources.

- Reading and Literacy Improvement: AI applications such as Readable can analyse a child's reading patterns, suggest suitable books, and even help improve reading skills by providing interactive reading experiences.

- Development of Critical Thinking and Problem-Solving: AI-driven puzzles and problem-solving games can help develop children's critical thinking and analytical skills by presenting them with challenges that require logical reasoning and creativity.

- Mathematics Tutoring: AI-powered platforms like Photomath allow children to receive instant help with maths problems. The app can solve problems using the smartphone's camera and explain the solutions step-by-step.

- Science Learning Tools: AI tools can simulate scientific experiments and models, providing a practical understanding of theoretical scientific concepts that might be difficult to grasp.

- Speech and Language Therapy: For children with speech or language difficulties, AI-powered tools can provide practice exercises and track progress in pronunciation, fluency, and language usage.

- AI for Special Education: AI can offer customised learning experiences for children with special needs, adapting to their unique learning requirements and helping them to develop their strengths.

- Coding and Robotics: Platforms like Scratch or Tynker use AI to teach children coding and robotics interactively and engagingly, preparing them for a future in a technology-driven world.

- Cultural and Global Awareness: AI-driven educational content can expose children to different cultures and global issues, promoting a broader understanding of the world.

Several other learning platforms for kids have gained popularity due to their engaging content, adaptability to individual learning styles, and effectiveness in complementing traditional education. Here are some of the most popular ones: ABCMouse, IXL Learning, Epic!, Adventure Academy, Raz-Kids, BrainPOP and SplashLearn.

By integrating AI in these various forms, children's education and development can be significantly enhanced, providing them with a more personalised, engaging, and practical learning experience.

2.3. Fitness and Health for the Family

AI's role in health and fitness can be instrumental in maintaining a healthy lifestyle for you and your family. Here are detailed ways in which AI can be beneficial in this aspect.

AI-driven fitness apps and platforms can create customised workout routines based on individual family members' fitness levels, goals, and preferences. Many fitness apps in the market are popular for their personalised, AI-driven features. Here are some of the notable ones:

- Future is an app which combines the best personal training with the flexibility to work out anytime, anywhere. It pairs you with a coach who will design a personalised workout plan. This is one of the best personal trainer apps because it's a fitness app for those who want a fully customised experience. Future has a wide variety of coaches, which is especially good for beginners who need guidance in specific areas and those who want a coach specialising in particular workouts.

- Caliber is one of the best personal trainer apps for variety because it offers users a one-on-one, virtual personal training experience with diversified and tailored workouts. It also provides nutritional guidance to help crush goals more quickly. You'll match with a certified trainer who will create new workouts for you weekly, guaranteeing you'll never be bored with your training.

- Joggo is appropriate for beginners, elite runners and everyone in between. It will create a personalised running plan depending on your fitness level and goals. This running app will create a customised running routine and meal plan to help you meet your competitive goals and wellness targets.

- MyFitnessPal is widely known for its comprehensive food database and nutrition tracking, MyFitnessPal also offers personalised workout routines. Its AI-driven features help track calorie intake and suggest meals based on individual goals.

- Nike Training Club provides a variety of workouts catering to different fitness levels and preferences. It includes AI-driven personal training plans that adapt to the user's progress and feedback.

- Fitbit App is best known for its wearable fitness trackers, the Fitbit app offers personalised workout routines, sleep tracking, and nutrition advice.

Its AI capabilities enhance the monitoring of physical activities and health metrics.

- Noom is unique for its psychological approach to fitness and weight loss, Noom uses AI to provide personalised meal plans and coaching. It focuses on making sustainable lifestyle changes.

- Aaptiv offers thousands of workouts focusing on audio coaching, Aaptiv uses AI to suggest workouts based on the user's fitness level and goals. It's great for mothers who prefer guided exercises without watching a screen.

- Freeletics is known for bodyweight workouts that require minimal equipment. It uses AI to create personalised fitness plans based on user feedback and progress.

- 8fit combines fitness, nutrition, and sleep tracking, 8fit offers personalised workout and meal plans. Its AI-driven approach is tailored to individual health and fitness goals.

- Centr by Chris Hemsworth provides a holistic approach to fitness, including workouts, meal plans, and mindfulness exercises. Its personal planner adapts to the user's lifestyle and goals.

- Jillian Michaels Fitness App offers personalised fitness programs and meal plans. It's great for mothers looking for structured, goal-oriented fitness routines.

- Sweat was founded by Kayla Itsines, this app is popular among women and includes workouts for different fitness levels, post-pregnancy workouts, and nutrition guidance.

- Strava is primarily known for tracking cycling and running activities, Strava uses AI to provide detailed analytics, performance tracking, and personalised challenges. It's popular among outdoor fitness enthusiasts.

- Peloton is famous for its at-home spin classes, Peloton also offers a variety of other workouts like strength training, yoga, and more. The app provides personalised workout recommendations based on user preferences and workout history.

- Daily Burn offers various workouts tailored to different fitness levels and goals. The app provides personalised daily workout plans and has a vital community aspect.

- Calm is primarily a meditation app. It includes mindful movement and gentle stretching exercises. It personalises recommendations based on user interactions and preferences.

- Headspace offers guided meditation sessions and has recently expanded to include workouts and movement exercises. The app uses AI to suggest personalised mindfulness and meditation routines.

- FitOn provides personalised fitness plans with workouts led by celebrity trainers. The app adapts to the user's fitness level and schedule preferences.

- Glo specialises in yoga, Pilates, and meditation, it offers tailored class recommendations based on the user's experience level and goals.

- MapMyRun by Under Armour is an app designed primarily for runners, this app tracks and maps out runs and offers personalised training plans, gear tracks, and social features.

- Asana Rebel focuses on yoga-inspired workouts, it provides personalised fitness routines and tracks user progress. It's known for its high-quality video content.

- Zwift combines fitness with gaming, it is an online platform that allows cyclists and runners to train and compete in a virtual environment. The app provides structured workouts and races with a vital community aspect.

Each of these apps caters to specific aspects of fitness and wellness, offering varied features from meditation and yoga to high-intensity workouts and outdoor activity tracking. They are great examples of how AI and personalisation can enhance the fitness app experience. These fitness apps are great for mothers, especially those looking for effective ways to balance their health, fitness, and parenting responsibilities.

Diet and Nutrition Planning: AI can analyse dietary preferences, nutritional needs, and health goals to suggest customised meal plans for family members.

Sleep Quality Improvement: AI-powered sleep tracking devices and apps can monitor sleep patterns, providing insights and suggestions to improve sleep quality. Devices like Fitbit or apps like Sleep Cycle analyse sleep stages and offer advice on achieving a more restful sleep, which is crucial for overall health.

Health Monitoring and Alerts: Wearable devices equipped with AI, such as smartwatches, can monitor vital signs like heart rate and blood pressure. They can alert users to potential health issues, encouraging timely medical consultations.

Mental Health Support: AI-driven mental health apps, like Woebot or Wysa, use cognitive-behavioural techniques to support stress, anxiety, and depression. These apps can offer personalised conversations and activities to help improve mental well-being.

Habit Formation and Tracking: AI can assist in forming and tracking healthy habits for the entire family. Apps like Habitica gamify habit formation, making it fun and engaging to stick to wholesome routines.

Chronic Disease Management: For families dealing with chronic health conditions, AI can aid in management by tracking symptoms and medication adherence and offering personalised advice. Apps like Quin use AI to assist people with diabetes in managing insulin levels.

AI in Physical Therapy: For those undergoing physical therapy, AI-driven software can guide exercises at home, ensuring correct form and adherence to therapeutic routines.

Interactive Fitness for Children: AI-powered fitness platforms for kids can make exercise fun and engaging through interactive games and activities that encourage physical activity.

Educational Content on Health: AI-driven content platforms can provide educational resources on various health topics tailored to family members' interests and needs, fostering a better understanding of health and wellness.

Remote Health Consultations: AI-powered telehealth services can facilitate remote consultations with healthcare providers, offering convenience for routine check-ups or essential medical advice.

Activity and Progress Tracking: Many AI fitness apps have features to track progress over time, offering insights and motivation to keep family members engaged in their health and fitness journey.

By leveraging these AI applications, families can significantly improve their approach to fitness and health, leading to a healthier lifestyle customised to each member's unique needs.

2.4. Ensuring Safety and Security

Artificial Intelligence (AI) can play a significant role in ensuring safety and security. Here are detailed examples of how AI can play a crucial role in this aspect:

Smart Home Security Systems: AI-powered home security systems like Ring or Nest use intelligent cameras and sensors to monitor a home's perimeter. These systems can differentiate between everyday activities and potential threats, such as an unrecognised person loitering near the property, and alert homeowners instantly through their smartphones.

Facial Recognition Technology: Some advanced home security cameras incorporate facial recognition technology. This feature allows the system to identify known family members and frequent visitors and alert the homeowner if an unknown individual is detected.

AI in Fire and Hazard Detection: AI can enhance traditional smoke and carbon monoxide detectors by analysing data trends to predict and prevent potential hazards. For instance, a smart smoke detector can identify the presence of smoke and analyse air quality for unusual patterns, alerting homeowners to potential fire hazards even before they escalate.

Cybersecurity for Home Networks: AI plays a critical role in cybersecurity with the increasing number of connected devices in homes. AI systems can monitor network traffic for unusual patterns, detect potential cyber threats, and protect sensitive data from hackers.

Child Safety Monitoring: AI-powered baby monitors and cameras can keep an eye on children, even in different rooms. These devices can detect unusual sounds or movements, like a baby's cry or a toddler attempting to climb out of the crib, and immediately alert parents.

Elder Care Assistance: For families with elderly members, AI-driven devices can offer additional safety measures. Wearable AI devices can detect falls and automatically call for help. Similarly, AI-assisted living systems can monitor the daily activities of elderly individuals, ensuring their safety and well-being.

AI for Pool Safety: AI technology also prevents drowning accidents in pools. Systems equipped with cameras and AI algorithms can monitor the pool area and detect if someone is struggling in the water, instantly alerting homeowners or emergency services.

Automated Emergency Services Contact: Some AI systems can contact emergency services automatically in an emergency. For example, if a break-in or fire is detected, the system can alert local police or fire departments, providing a faster response time.

Online Safety for Children: AI tools can help monitor a child's online activities, protecting them from potential dangers like cyberbullying, inappropriate content, or online predators. Parental control software with AI can analyse websites visited, time spent online, and social media interactions to ensure a safe online environment for children.

Natural Disaster Predictions and Alerts: AI algorithms can analyse vast amounts of data to accurately predict natural disasters like earthquakes, floods, or storms. AI-driven apps can provide families with early warnings and safety instructions, helping them to prepare and respond effectively.

By incorporating these AI technologies, families can significantly enhance their safety and security measures, ensuring a more secure and protected home environment.

Integrating AI into your daily life as a full-time mother isn't about overhauling your lifestyle but enhancing it. Adopting AI tools and technologies makes everyday tasks more efficient, supports your children's education, maintains your family's health and fitness, and ensures their safety and well-being. The following chapters will explore how AI can aid personal growth, manage finances, and even start a home-based business.

Chapter 3: AI Safety for Children: Navigating the Digital World

As Artificial Intelligence (AI) becomes increasingly integrated into our daily lives, it is crucial to understand its impact on one of the most vulnerable sections of society - our children. Children interact with AI in various ways, often without realising it.

This chapter provides a comprehensive overview of AI's impact on children, balancing its educational and entertainment benefits with potential risks and offering strategies for responsible and effective use.

3.1. AI's Role in Enhancing Learning and Development

Many educational tools and apps use AI to provide a personalised learning experience. AI algorithms can adapt to a child's unique learning style and pace, offering customised content in maths, language, and science. Here are some of the most popular ones.

Educational Tools and Apps:

- Khan Academy is known for its comprehensive learning resources. It uses AI to offer personalised maths, science, and humanities learning paths.

- Duolingo is a language learning platform that uses AI to adapt lessons to the learner's ability, ensuring that the pace and content are suitable for their level of proficiency.

- Quizlet is an AI-powered study tool that provides personalised learning experiences through flashcards, quizzes, and games, adapting to the student's study habits and progress.

- Prodigy Math Game is a game-based learning app that uses AI to tailor maths questions to each child's learning level, making maths fun and engaging.

- IXL Learning offers a comprehensive K-12 curriculum with AI-driven recommendations based on the student's performance, providing personalised practice in maths, language arts, science, and social studies.

- CuriosityStream is a streaming service offering educational videos and documentaries. It uses AI to suggest content based on viewing history and preferences.

- Socratic by Google is an AI-powered homework help app that provides explanations, videos, and step-by-step assistance in various subjects tailored to the student's questions.

- Epic! is an extensive digital library for kids under 12. It uses AI to suggest books and videos tailored to the child's interests and reading level.

- Brainly is a community-based learning app where students ask and answer questions. AI is used to match questions with the right experts and to provide educational resources.

- Rosetta Stone is a language learning app that uses AI in its TruAccent speech-recognition engine to provide feedback on pronunciation, helping learners to speak accurately.

These apps leverage AI to create adaptive learning environments, making education more engaging, personalised, and effective for children. They cover a range of subjects and skills, from maths and science to languages and general knowledge. AI's ability to create personalised and interactive experiences keeps children engaged and motivated to explore and learn.

Voice-Activated Assistants: Devices like Amazon Echo (Alexa), Google Home, Siri and Samsung's Bixby are popular in households and use AI to understand and respond to voice commands. Children might use these devices to play music, ask questions for homework, or set reminders.

Interactive Toys and Games: Some AI-powered toys and games can respond to children's actions and words, providing an interactive and engaging play experience. These toys can adapt and change behaviour based on how the child plays with them.

Content Recommendations: Streaming services like Netflix or YouTube use AI to recommend videos and movies based on previous viewing habits. Children experience this when they receive suggestions for shows similar to those they have watched.

Safety and Monitoring Tools: Some AI applications help parents monitor their children's online activity and usage patterns to ensure safety and appropriate content.

In all these interactions, AI can be a tool for learning, entertainment, and safety for children. AI-based toy and game-based learning can complement traditional teaching methods, providing parents and educators with valuable data insights and assessment tools to monitor children's progress and tailor instruction. However, it's also crucial for parents to monitor and guide their children's interaction with AI to ensure a balanced and safe digital experience.

3.2. The Entertainment Value of AI for Children

AI plays a significant role in children's games, creating more interactive and engaging experiences. Here's how AI is utilised in this context:

Adaptive Difficulty Levels: AI algorithms can adjust the difficulty level of a game based on the player's performance. Suppose a child finds a level too easy or too challenging. In that case, the game can adapt in real-time to provide an appropriate level of difficulty, keeping the game both challenging and enjoyable.

Personalised Learning Experiences: In educational games, AI tracks the child's progress and identifies areas of strength and weakness. The game can then tailor its content to focus on areas needing improvement, thus offering a personalised learning journey.

Interactive and Responsive Gameplay: AI enables game characters to respond dynamically to the child's actions and choices, making the gameplay more interactive and authentic. For example, characters might learn from the player's previous decisions and react differently in future scenarios.

Natural Language Processing (NLP): Games that use voice recognition allow children to interact with the game using spoken language. NLP, a field of AI, helps understand and process the child's speech, enabling games to respond meaningfully.

Here are some popular types of games that incorporate NLP: Text-based adventure games like "AI Dungeon", educational language games like "Duolingo" and "Rosetta Stone", voice-controlled games like "There Came an Echo" and AI chatbot games like "Event[0]".

Enhancing Creativity: Some AI-driven games provide creative platforms where children can build or create scenarios. The AI can suggest improvements, offer ideas, or even autonomously create alongside the child, enhancing their creative experience. AI-driven games that offer creative platforms for children to build or create scenarios are becoming increasingly popular as they blend entertainment with

educational aspects like problem-solving, creativity, and coding skills. Here are some notable examples:

1. Minecraft with AI Mods: Minecraft is inherently a creative game where players build and explore virtual worlds. The game can be enhanced with AI mods to include intelligent NPCs or automate specific tasks, providing a more interactive and creative experience.

2. Roblox: This is a platform where kids can design their games and play games created by others. Roblox Studio, the game development suite for Roblox, allows for incorporating AI elements in these custom games, enabling children to experiment with AI-driven scenarios.

3. Scratch: Developed by MIT, Scratch is an educational platform that teaches children how to code. While it's not an AI-driven game per se, it allows kids to create games, animations, and interactive stories and can be a stepping stone to understanding AI concepts.

4. LEGO Mindstorms: This platform combines traditional LEGO building with computer programming. Kids can build their LEGO robots and program them to perform various tasks, offering a tangible way to experiment with AI and robotics.

5. Tynker: Tynker is an educational platform that teaches children coding. It offers various modules, some of which involve AI and machine learning concepts, allowing kids to create games and animations using these technologies.

6. Kodu Game Lab: Developed by Microsoft, Kodu is a visual programming tool which allows kids to create games on the PC and Xbox. It includes AI programming concepts, enabling children to incorporate intelligent characters and scenarios in their games.

7. Osmo: Osmo is an educational game system integrating physical play with digital apps, encouraging creativity and problem-solving skills. Some of its games involve AI-driven activities, blending the physical and virtual worlds.

8. Lightbot: A puzzle game that introduces kids to programming logic. While not directly AI-driven, it teaches the basics of sequencing, procedures, and loops, which are fundamental concepts in AI.

These platforms not only entertain but also educate, providing children with an early understanding of AI, programming, and creative problem-solving. They are instrumental in fostering an interest in technology and innovation from a young age.

Behavioural Pattern Recognition: AI analyses how a child plays a game, recognising patterns in their behaviour. This information can be used to customise game experiences, like suggesting new game levels, challenges, or educational content that aligns with the child's interests and play style.

Emotion Recognition: Advanced games employ AI-driven emotion recognition through facial expression analysis or voice tone. This can adjust the game's narrative or difficulty based on the child's emotional response, ensuring an engaging experience.

Safety and Moderation: AI also monitors online interactions in children's games to ensure a safe gaming environment. It can filter out inappropriate content and manage interactions to prevent cyberbullying.

Content Customisation: Discuss how AI algorithms customise entertainment content, such as movie suggestions on streaming platforms, based on previous viewing history.

By incorporating these AI capabilities, children's games have evolved into more than just entertainment; they have become dynamic platforms that offer personalised, adaptive, and educational experiences. This makes the games more engaging and enhances their potential as tools for learning and creative expression.

3.3. Potential Risks and Challenges

While AI offers numerous benefits in enhancing children's learning and entertainment experiences, it also presents certain risks and challenges that parents and educators should be aware of. Minimising the risks imposed by AI, especially for children, is crucial for parents and educators. Adopting these strategies can help to ensure a safe and beneficial interaction with AI technologies.

Parents and educators should educate themselves and then teach children about AI. This includes understanding its capabilities, limitations, and ethical considerations.

What AI is and how it works is the first step. We should encourage children to think critically about their information and interactions with AI. This includes questioning the sources of information and understanding that AI-generated responses may not always be accurate or appropriate. Parents can consider setting boundaries and usage limits. It's essential to set clear guidelines for how and when AI technologies can be used. This includes limiting screen time and ensuring that AI interactions are appropriate for the child's age and maturity level.

It is our responsibility to teach children about online privacy and data security. Explain how AI systems use data, the importance of protecting personal information, and how to manage privacy settings on different platforms. It's essential to keep an eye on the AI platforms and tools children are using. This can be done through direct supervision or parental control software. Engage with them about their experiences and what they're learning. It is also important to discuss the ethical use of AI, such as respecting others' privacy, understanding bias in AI systems, and the importance of using AI for positive purposes.

Parents can choose age-appropriate AI tools by selecting AI-based educational tools and games suitable for the child's age and developmental stage. Look for products that have a good reputation for safety and educational value. We must aim to foster a balanced approach. While AI can be a powerful tool for learning and entertainment, it's important to balance its use with non-digital activities. Encourage physical play, outdoor activities, and face-to-face social interactions.

AI technology is rapidly evolving. Parents and educators should stay informed about the latest developments in AI and the emerging concerns associated with its use. We can work with schools and community groups to develop policies and practices for AI's safe and ethical use in educational settings.

By taking these steps, parents can help ensure that children benefit from AI technologies while minimising potential risks. It's about creating a balanced, informed, safe environment for children to explore and learn. It's also vital for parents to model good digital habits and foster open communication about the technology their children are using. Regular discussions about the responsible use of technology can also be beneficial.

3.4. Balancing AI Interaction

Setting boundaries to balance children's interaction with AI involves a thoughtful approach that considers the child's age, maturity, and the specific AI technologies they are using. Here are steps parents can take to create a healthy balance:

- Educate Yourself and Your Child: Understand the basics of AI and the specific technologies your child is using. Educate your child about AI, how it works, its benefits, and potential risks.

- Establish Clear Rules: Set specific rules for AI usage. This includes when and where AI technologies can be used, for how long, and for what purposes. Make these rules consistent and enforce them fairly.

- Monitor Content and Usage: Keep track of what AI applications and devices your child is using. Ensure the content is age-appropriate and the interactions are safe. Use parental control tools if necessary.

- Encourage Critical Thinking: Teach your child to question and critically evaluate their interactions with AI. Discuss how AI might influence their thinking or behaviour and the importance of forming their opinions.

- Promote Privacy Awareness: Educate your child about online privacy. Teach them not to share personal information and be cautious about the data they generate using AI technologies.

- Balance Screen Time with Other Activities: Encourage non-screen activities like reading, physical play, and family time. Ensure that your child has a healthy balance between digital and real-world experiences.

- Foster Emotional Intelligence: Help your child understand the difference between human interaction and AI. Encourage empathy, social skills, and emotional understanding, which AI interactions cannot provide.

- Create Tech-Free Zones and Times: Establish certain areas in the home, like bedrooms or dining areas, as tech-free zones. Also, designate tech-free times, such as family meals or before bedtime.

- Model Good Behaviour: Children often imitate their parents' behaviour. Show a balanced approach to technology in your own life to set a positive example.

- Stay Informed and Flexible: AI technology is constantly evolving. Keep yourself updated and be flexible to adjust rules and boundaries as necessary.

- Open Communication: Maintain open lines of communication. Talk regularly with your child about their experiences and learnings from AI interactions. This helps in understanding their perspective and addressing any issues that arise.

- Educational Use: Encourage the use of AI for educational purposes. Guide them towards AI tools that promote learning and creativity.

By implementing these steps, parents can help their children navigate the world of AI safely and responsibly, ensuring that their interactions with AI are enriching and appropriately balanced.

AI offers vast opportunities for children's growth and learning but also presents unique challenges. As parents and guardians, understanding AI's role in children's lives is crucial for maximising its benefits while mitigating risks. By being informed and proactive, we can ensure that AI positively influences our children's development. By harnessing AI effectively, we can create a future where children's curiosity and imagination are nurtured, and learning becomes a joyful and fulfilling experience that prepares them to thrive in an ever-changing world.

Appendix

Online Safety Tools and Resources:

Family Online Safety Institute (FOSI)

- Provides resources for parents to help ensure children's safety online.

- fosi.org

Common Sense Media

- Offers independent reviews, age ratings, and other information about all types of media for parents and children.

- Commonsensemedia.org

NetSmartz

- Educational program from the National Center for Missing & Exploited Children that provides resources to help teach children how to be safer on- and offline.

- netsmartz.org

Parental Control Software:

Qustodio

- A comprehensive parental control software that offers a range of features including internet filtering, time controls, and monitoring.
- qustodio.com

Bark

- Monitors texts, email, YouTube, and 30+ social networks for potential safety concerns, so parents can save time and gain peace of mind.
- bark.us

Kaspersky Safe Kids

- Helps you manage and monitor device usage, set rules for internet access, and see what your kids are doing online.
- kaspersky.com/safe-kids

Educational Resources for Children about AI and Online Safety:

"Be Internet Awesome" by Google

- A program that teaches kids the fundamentals of digital citizenship and safety so they can explore the online world with confidence.
- beinternetawesome.withgoogle.com

BrainPOP

- Animated Educational Site for Kids offering resources on technology, digital citizenship, and more.
- brainpop.com

Code.org

- Offers coding lessons for children and also includes modules on digital citizenship and AI basics.
- code.org

Books for Parents and Children:

"Raising Humans in a Digital World: Helping Kids Build a Healthy Relationship with Technology" by Diana Graber

- Offers practical advice to help parents teach their children how to be safe, healthy, and responsible in the digital world.

"Screenwise: Helping Kids Thrive (and Survive) in Their Digital World" by Devorah Heitner

- A guide for parents on how to mentor their kids in the digital age, with a focus on helping them build essential skills.

"The Art of Screen Time: How Your Family Can Balance Digital Media and Real Life" by Anya Kamenetz

- Explores how families can make thoughtful decisions about screens and digital media.

These resources provide comprehensive support for parents and children navigating AI and digital landscapes, offering tools for safety, education, and responsible use of technology.

Chapter 4: Personal Growth and AI

Harnessing AI for Your Personal Development

As a full-time mother, finding time for personal growth can be challenging. This chapter delves into how AI can catalyse personal development, helping mothers balance their multifaceted roles with their aspirations for growth.

4.1. AI-Driven Learning and Skill Development

Expanding your knowledge and skills is crucial for personal fulfilment and potential career advancement. Several popular online learning platforms offer various courses and resources for full-time mothers looking to expand their knowledge and skills for personal fulfilment or potential career advancement. Many AI-powered platforms are offering various courses, from digital marketing to health and wellness, tailored to your interests and schedule. These flexible platforms allow for learning at your own pace, which is particularly convenient for those with busy schedules. Here are some of the top platforms:

1. Coursera: Offers courses from universities and organisations worldwide. Topics range from business and technology to personal development and art. Many courses are free, with options to pay for certification.

2. Udemy: Features a vast array of courses on web development, digital marketing, personal development, art, and more. Udemy often has sales, making courses quite affordable.

3. Khan Academy: A free resource that provides courses primarily in maths, science, and computing but also includes lessons in arts and humanities, economics, and more. It's well-suited for brushing up on fundamental skills or learning alongside your children.

4. LinkedIn Learning (formerly Lynda.com): Offers video courses by industry experts in business, creative and technology skills. It's an excellent resource for learning new professional skills or upgrading existing ones.

5. edX: Provides access to courses from universities like Harvard, MIT, and others. Courses cover a wide range of topics, from computer science to philosophy, and many courses are free to audit.

6. Skillshare: Focuses on creative courses like illustration, photography, design, and more. It's great for mothers interested in exploring their creativity or developing new artistic skills.

7. MasterClass: Offers classes taught by celebrities and renowned figures in their fields. If you're interested in learning cooking from Gordon Ramsay or writing from Margaret Atwood, this platform is for you.

8. Codecademy: Excellent for those interested in learning coding. Offers interactive courses on web development, programming, data science, and more.

9. FutureLearn: Offers courses from universities and cultural institutions around the world. They have many topics, including business, healthcare, and arts.

10. Pluralsight: Focuses on tech-oriented courses, especially in software development, IT operations, and cybersecurity. It is ideal for those looking to enter or advance in the tech industry.

These platforms cater to various interests and career goals, whether you're looking to gain new skills for a potential job, start a business, or explore areas of personal interest. The flexibility and breadth of courses available make them ideal for full-time mothers who need to fit learning into a busy schedule.

Language learning apps have become increasingly popular due to their convenience and innovative learning methods. Here are some of the most popular language-learning apps on the market:

1. Duolingo: Known for its game-like lessons, Duolingo offers a user-friendly and fun way to learn many languages. It's great for beginners and provides reading, writing, listening, and speaking practice.

2. Babbel: This app focuses on conversational learning and grammar. It's designed to get learners to speak their new language quickly and offers courses tailored to each language's unique grammatical quirks.

3. Rosetta Stone: A long-established leader in language learning, Rosetta Stone uses immersive methods, teaching languages in the context of complete sentences and real-life situations without relying on translation to one's native language.

4. Memrise: Memrise uses spaced repetition and mnemonic techniques to help learners memorise new vocabulary and phrases. It also uses videos of native speakers to provide context for how language is used in real life.

5. Busuu: Offering interactive language courses and a community feature for getting feedback from native speakers, Busuu also allows learners to practise speaking and writing skills.

6. HelloTalk: This app connects learners with native speakers around the world. Users can chat with native speakers, correct each other's messages, and learn by immersing themselves in the language.

7. Pimsleur: Pimsleur is audio-focused and significant for learners interested in improving their listening and speaking skills. It uses spaced repetition and encourages learners from the first lesson to speak aloud.

8. Tandem: Similar to HelloTalk, Tandem is a language exchange app where users can connect with native speakers of their target language and practice by texting and speaking.

9. Lingodeer: This app is perfect for learning Asian languages. It offers detailed grammar explanations and a variety of exercises, catering to different learning styles.

10. Mango Languages: Offers a wide variety of languages and focuses on practical, real-world conversations and insights into the culture of the language being learnt.

These learning platforms cater to different learning styles and goals, whether gaining conversational skills, learning through immersion, or focusing on grammar and vocabulary. Many offer free versions, while some require a subscription for full access. Discover how AI-driven apps make learning a new language more effective and fun with personalised lessons and interactive exercises.

Skill Enhancement Tools: Learn about AI tools to help you improve specific skills, such as writing, public speaking, or artistic pursuits.

Developing writing skills can be significantly aided by various apps, each offering unique features to enhance different aspects of writing. Here are some of the most popular apps that can help mothers (and anyone else) improve their writing skills:

1. Grammarly: This AI-powered tool is excellent for correcting grammar, spelling, and punctuation mistakes. It also offers suggestions to improve clarity, style and tone, making it useful for casual and professional writing.

2. Hemingway Editor: This app focuses on making your writing bold and clear. This editor emphasises and amends grammar, fluency, and sentence construction, enhancing the readability and appearance of your writing.

3. Scrivener: Particularly useful for long-form writing projects like novels or research papers, Scrivener helps organise and manage complex writing projects. It's great for structuring your thoughts and ideas.

4. Evernote: Ideal for note-taking and organising your thoughts and ideas, Evernote helps you capture and prioritise ideas, projects, and to-do lists, ensuring nothing falls through the cracks.

5. Google Docs: This is an excellent tool for collaborative writing. This tool enables you to compose, modify, and work with others from anywhere. The real-time collaboration feature is handy for getting feedback.

6. Reedsy: Offers a clean, distraction-free interface for writing. It's perfect for book writing and provides access to a community of writers and publishing professionals.

7. Ulysses: A popular app among Apple users, Ulysses offers a distraction-free writing environment and is excellent for managing multiple writing projects efficiently.

8. ProWritingAid: This writing tool offers in-depth writing analysis, which is more comprehensive than simple grammar checking. It helps improve readability, style, and tone.

9. Microsoft Word: An old favourite, Microsoft Word's newer versions include features like Editor, which provides advanced spelling, grammar, and stylistic writing suggestions.

10. FocusWriter: Designed to help you focus on writing by removing distractions. It provides a clean, distraction-free writing environment, which can be particularly helpful for mothers seeking to make the most of limited writing time.

Each app offers unique functionalities that cater to different writing needs, from correcting grammatical errors to organising thoughts and ideas. They can be invaluable for mothers looking to hone their writing skills, whether for personal, professional, or creative writing.

Improving public speaking skills can be valuable for anyone, including mothers. Fortunately, there are several apps designed to help enhance these skills. Here are some of the most popular ones:

1. Orai: This AI-powered app offers feedback on your speech clarity, pace, use of filler words, and energy. It provides detailed analytics on your speech and helps you practise and improve over time.

2. VirtualSpeech: A VR app that provides a realistic environment for practising public speaking. It offers feedback on your performance, including eye contact, rate of speech, and use of filler words.

3. Speeko: This app provides AI-driven feedback on your speaking skills, including pacing, tone, and clarity. It also offers exercises to improve areas like articulation and breath control.

4. Toastmasters Pathfinder: While not an app, Toastmasters International offers a program called Pathways, an excellent resource for improving public speaking. They also provide local club meetings for practising general speaking skills.

5. Ummo: This app is your personal speech coach and provides detailed analytics on your speech, such as filler words, pace, and clarity. It's helpful in practising speeches and presentations.

6. LikeSo: Offers a personal speech coach experience, focusing on reducing filler words and improving articulation. It's great for practising for interviews, presentations, or everyday conversations.

7. VoiceVibes: This app uses AI to analyse your speech and offers feedback on how you come across, whether confident, precise, or authentic. It helps in refining the way you present your speech.

8. Public Speaking for Cardboard: A VR app that simulates a public speaking environment to practise presentations. It helps overcome stage fright and improve speaking skills.

9. Prompster: Acts as a teleprompter and speech preparation tool, helping you practise delivering speeches and presentations without stumbling over words.

10. SpeakApp: Records and analyses your speeches, providing feedback on various aspects like speed, pauses, volume, and emotion to help you improve your public speaking skills.

These apps can be particularly beneficial for busy mothers who may not have the time to attend in-person public speaking courses. They offer the flexibility to practise and improve at their own pace and in their own space.

When considering drawing and painting apps suitable for mothers, especially those who might be balancing childcare with personal hobbies or looking to explore their artistic side, it's crucial to choose user-friendly, versatile apps that offer a good range of features without being overwhelming. Here are some popular options:

1. Procreate: Highly recommended for iPad users, Procreate is intuitive and offers a wide range of brushes and tools. It's great for both beginners and professional artists, with the ability to create stunning artwork.

2. Adobe Fresco: Known for its natural drawing and painting experience, Adobe Fresco is suitable for all skill levels. It offers a mix of raster and vector brushes and integrates well with other Adobe apps, making it a good choice for those who might also use Adobe Creative Cloud.

3. Autodesk SketchBook: This app is user-friendly and offers professional-grade tools. It's a good option for mothers looking for a straightforward but powerful drawing tool. It's available on both iOS and Android devices.

4. ArtFlow: An Android app that is easy to use and has a simple interface, ArtFlow is excellent for mothers new to digital art. It provides a variety of brushes and tools, and the basic version is free.

5. Ibis Paint X: Known for its smooth drawing experience, ibis Paint X is popular among amateur and professional artists. It's user-friendly, making it suitable for mothers who are beginners in digital art. Available on iOS and Android.

6. MediBang Paint: This app is lightweight and offers a variety of brushes, fonts, and premade backgrounds. It's great for creating digital paintings and comics and available on multiple platforms.

7. Adobe Photoshop Sketch: For those familiar with Adobe products, this app offers a range of Photoshop brushes and is compatible with iOS and Android. It's great for sketching and painting.

8. Tayasui Sketches: Known for its beautiful and user-friendly interface, this app offers a variety of brushes and tools. It's a good choice for mothers who want a simple yet powerful tool for sketching and painting.

9. Paper by WeTransfer: Focused on simplicity and ease of use, Paper is excellent for quick sketches, drawings, and note-taking. It's available on iOS and is particularly user-friendly for beginners.

10. Concepts: An advanced sketching and design app, Concepts is suitable for those interested in more technical drawing. It offers an infinite canvas and a natural drawing experience. It's available on iOS, Windows, and Android.

These apps cater to various artistic interests and skill levels, from casual doodling to more severe art projects. Many offer free versions or trials, which can be a good starting point for mothers looking to explore digital art.

4.2. Mental Health and Well-Being

A fascinating but frightening process begins in their bodies and psyches when women become mothers. Ninety per cent of women experience some mood disorder during motherhood. Twenty-five per cent of women suffer from severe maternal mental health pathology. Dealing with kids and family is one of the most challenging tasks for parents. Our kids need us alive and in good health. That's why we must care for our mental and physical health at all costs.

AI offers tools to support your mental well-being. Meditation and mindfulness apps are excellent tools for mothers seeking relaxation, stress reduction, and a moment of calm in their busy lives. Here are some popular meditation and mindfulness apps that cater to a variety of preferences and needs:

- Headspace: Known for its friendly, approachable style, Headspace offers guided meditations, mindfulness exercises, and sleep stories. It's great for beginners and includes special sessions for moments of panic, anxiety, and stress.

- Calm: This app is famous for its relaxing soundscapes, guided meditations, and bedtime stories (including ones read by celebrities). It covers many topics, from stress relief to focus and self-esteem.

- Insight Timer: Offering the most extensive free library of guided meditations, Insight Timer has thousands of sessions on various topics. It also features a customisable timer for unguided meditation.

- 10% Happier: This app employs direct language and humour to assist you in improving sleep, lowering stress levels, and enhancing your focus. It features a variety of meditation courses tailored to different aspects of life, including parenting.

- Smiling Mind: Developed by psychologists, Smiling Mind offers programs for different age groups and goals, including programs specifically for parents.

- Buddhify: This app is designed for on-the-go meditation and mindfulness. It offers sessions that fit into any schedule, such as during a work break or waiting in line.

- MyLife Meditation (formerly Stop, Breathe & Think): This is an award-winning app personalised to how you feel. It encourages users to check in with their emotions and recommends short, guided meditations and activities tuned to how they feel.

- Simple Habit: Designed for busy people, Simple Habit offers meditations as short as 5 minutes, making it perfect for moms on the go. It covers a range of topics, including meditation for parenting.

- Sattva: Rooted in Vedic principles, Sattva offers a range of meditations, chants, and mantras. It also includes a meditation timer and insights into your progress.

- The Mindfulness App: Offers a range of guided and silent meditations and is suitable for beginners and experienced practitioners. It also includes mindfulness notices and stats to track your progress.

- Moodfit: This app offers tools to help shape your mood. Along with mood tracking, it provides activities and insights to help you understand and improve your mental health.

- Daylio: A versatile mood-tracking app that allows you to keep a private journal without typing a single line. It's straightforward and user-friendly, perfect for busy moms.

- Moodnotes: Designed to capture your mood and help you improve your thinking habits, Moodnotes is particularly useful for identifying trends in your emotions and managing stress and anxiety.

- Sanvello (formerly Pacifica): Provides clinically validated techniques and support to help you manage stress, anxiety, and depression. It offers mood tracking, coping tools, and community support.

- Reflectly: A journaling app that uses AI to help users to structure and reflect upon their daily thoughts and problems. It assists in tracking mood and identifying patterns.

- My Possible Self: An app that uses learning modules to help you manage fear, anxiety, and stress. It helps track your mood and teaches coping mechanisms.

- Happify: Designed to help you overcome negative thoughts and stress through science-based activities and games.

These apps are designed to fit into various lifestyles and schedules, making them suitable for mothers looking to incorporate meditation and mindfulness into their daily routines. Emotional health trackers can be beneficial for mothers in managing stress, tracking mood changes, and maintaining overall mental well-being. These apps often include features like mood tracking, journaling, and sometimes even AI-driven insights. Most offer free basic versions with the option of subscribing for full access to their content.

AI-powered therapy and counselling apps have become increasingly popular, offering accessible mental health support. These apps use artificial intelligence to provide guidance, therapeutic techniques, and emotional support. They can be beneficial for mothers seeking flexible and private mental health resources. Here are some popular options:

- Woebot: This app uses AI to provide therapeutic conversations based on cognitive behavioural therapy (CBT) principles. It helps users monitor their mood and learn about themselves through intelligent chat.

- Wysa: Combining AI-driven conversations with support from human therapists, Wysa offers tools to manage mental health, including anxiety and depression. The AI chatbot helps with stress, sleep, and resilience.

- Youper: This AI therapy app uses quick conversations to support mental health, incorporating techniques from CBT, Acceptance Commitment Therapy, and mindfulness. It also tracks mood and emotional health patterns.

- Replika: While not a therapy app per se, Replika uses AI to create a personal chatbot friend that can help users talk through their feelings and thoughts, providing emotional support and companionship.

- Headspace Care (Ginger): Offers access to emotional support through AI-assisted coaching and video therapy with licensed therapists. It's designed to provide immediate support and help users work through issues.

- Talkspace: Though primarily known for its access to licensed therapists, Talkspace also offers AI-driven features to help users manage their mental health, including tools for anxiety and depression.

- Sanvello (formerly Pacifica): Provides self-help tools, guided journeys, and the option to connect with licensed therapists. Its AI-driven features include mood tracking and cognitive-behavioural techniques.

- MoodKit: Developed by psychologists, this app uses AI to provide tools based on CBT principles to improve mood and mental health.

- Quirk CBT: An AI-powered app that helps in practising Cognitive Behavioral Therapy. It assists users in identifying and challenging distorted thoughts.

- MindDoc (formerly Moodpath): An AI-driven mental health companion app that screens for symptoms of depression, anxiety, and other mental conditions and provides therapeutic support.

These apps are not a replacement for professional therapy but can provide valuable support and tools for managing everyday stress, anxiety, and other mental health challenges. They are particularly beneficial for mothers needing flexible and immediate support tailored to their busy schedules.

4.3. Building Networks and Communities

Creating connections and building a supportive network is vital for personal growth and fulfilment. Social media and networking apps can be precious for mothers looking to create connections and build a supportive network. These platforms allow for establishing connections, sharing experiences, and finding support. Here are some popular social media and networking apps that are particularly useful for mothers:

1. Facebook: With its vast user base, Facebook makes it easy to join groups and communities of fellow mothers. There are numerous parenting groups where mothers can share advice, experiences, and support.

2. Instagram: An excellent platform for visually sharing life's moments. Mothers can follow parenting accounts, exchange personal stories and engage with a community of similar interests and perspectives.

3. WhatsApp: This messaging app helps create private chat groups. Mothers can use it to contact family, friends, and parenting groups.

4. Peanut: Explicitly designed for mothers and mothers-to-be, Peanut provides a platform to connect with other women for support, advice, and friendship. It's like a social network for moms.

5. Meetup: This app helps find local groups and events, which can be great for mothers looking to connect with other parents in their area. It offers various meet-up categories, including parenting and family groups.

6. LinkedIn: While known as a professional networking site, LinkedIn can also be useful for mothers seeking to connect with professional groups, join discussions, and even find flexible work opportunities.

7. Twitter: A platform where mothers can follow parenting experts, join conversations, and share their experiences and tips with a larger audience.

8. Pinterest: Ideal for mothers looking for inspiration, whether for parenting tips, crafts, recipes, or home organisation ideas. Pinterest also allows you to connect with other users and share ideas.

9. Nextdoor: A neighbourhood app that connects local communities, Nextdoor can be a valuable tool for mothers to learn about local events, sell or exchange items, and seek or offer support within their community.

10. Mom Life: A community app where moms can connect, share stories, seek advice, and find support from other mothers worldwide.

These apps offer a mix of social connection, information sharing, and community support, which can be particularly beneficial for mothers seeking to expand their social networks and find support from others who understand the joys and challenges of motherhood.

AI-powered event and activity finder apps can benefit mothers looking to discover local events, activities for kids, family-friendly outings, or even personal interests. These apps often use AI to personalise recommendations based on interests, location, and preferences. Here are some popular AI-powered event and activity finder apps:

1. Eventbrite: Offers a wide range of event listings from various categories. AI algorithms suggest events based on your past searches and interests.

2. Meetup: Utilises AI to recommend groups and events based on your interests. It's great for finding local groups focused on parenting, hobbies, or professional networking.

3. Hoop: Specifically designed for parents, Hoop uses AI to suggest family-friendly activities and events happening nearby, tailored to the ages of your children.

4. Google Local Guides: While not strictly an event finder, Google's AI-driven recommendations in Maps and Search can help you discover local activities, venues, and events based on your preferences and search history.

5. Nextdoor: This neighbourhood app connects you with your local community and uses AI to inform you about local events, community activities, and family-friendly gatherings.

6. Yelp: Known for business reviews, Yelp also uses AI to suggest events and activities based on your location and previous searches and reviews.

7. Kidadl: Specifically targeted at families, Kidadl provides personalised suggestions for child-friendly activities and events, leveraging AI to cater to your family's interests and the kids' ages.

8. ParentMap: This app and website offer many family activities and events resources, with personalised recommendations to suit your interests and needs.

9. Time Out: Discover events, activities, and places in your city. The app uses AI to tailor recommendations to your preferences and past activity.

These apps can significantly simplify finding exciting and appropriate events and activities for mothers and their families, offering personalised suggestions to save time and cater to specific interests.

4.4. Balancing Personal Time and Responsibilities

4.4.1. Time Management and Self-Care

Parenthood is a beautiful journey but comes with its fair share of challenges. Sleepless nights, endless diaper changes, school runs, and extracurricular activities can tire parents. Balancing these responsibilities while maintaining your identity and pursuing your passions can seem daunting.

Time Management

Efficient time management is the cornerstone of harmonising parenthood and self-care. Time management is a process that involves planning and organising tasks in order of importance and urgency. People can use their time effectively and productively through effective time management techniques. It is vital to develop time management skills to successfully achieve our goals. Several time management techniques can be used.

The POSEC method is one of the most popular time management techniques. POSEC stands for "Prioritising by Organising, Streamlining, Economising and Contributing".

The different role of the POSEC method is explained below:

1. Prioritising - This means that all the tasks assigned require prioritisation. It is essential to note down all the critical tasks. It also involves how you use your time to complete all your goals. Allocation of tasks must depend on the degree of priority.

2. Organising - After prioritising all your tasks, it is essential to organise them. This involves making a plan to achieve the goals you set out. This will allow an individual to feel more stable and secure. It is essential to follow the plan regularly to complete your tasks.

3. Streamlining - This aspect involves streamlining everything you don't like doing but must do. These tasks include jobs such as work or chores essential to function daily. Streamlining helps in managing and maintenance of personal stability and security.

4. Economising - This involves all the enjoyable things that must be done for recreation. These activities include socialising and engaging in different pastimes.

5. Contributing - Contributing involves what you give back to the community or the world. It is linked to social obligations that one must follow.

POSEC is a crucial time management technique that offers a straightforward guide on prioritising your goals in life.

The Eisenhower Method involves prioritising tasks according to their urgency. It helps to determine the essential activities that don't require attention. This time management technique was developed by Dwight D. Eisenhower. He said, "I have two kinds of problems: the urgent and the important. The urgent are not important, and the important are never urgent." It is also known as the Eisenhower matrix, one of the most widely used time management techniques globally.

The Eisenhower Matrix is categorised into 4 quadrants according to what one needs to do during the day. These quadrants are:

1. Do - The first quadrant of this time management technique, "do", consists of the most essential tasks you should do. These tasks need to be done urgently. It is considered urgent if the task needs to be done within a day or two.

2. Decide - The second quadrant of the Eisenhower method is "decide". It usually consists of tasks that are important but only sometimes urgent. A typical example is exercising regularly. We all know that it is beneficial to our health. But not everyone can dedicate time to it. Hence, it becomes essential to decide what time you should hit the gym or go for a run. Good time management techniques can go a long way in managing tasks efficiently.

3. Delegate - The third quadrant of this time management technique is "delegate". This category involves tasks that are not important but urgent. Even though the tasks may be necessary, it is optional for them to be compulsory. They don't contribute much towards productivity. Hence, it is up to you to decide whether you need to delegate or reschedule it.

4. Eliminate - The last quadrant of this matrix is "eliminate". These tasks do not contribute to the goals. So, identifying and eliminating these tasks is essential to ensure productivity. For example, surfing on social media or checking the phone constantly for messages.

Excellent time management means being effective as well as efficient. We must spend time doing essential tasks, not just the urgent ones.

Time management techniques are only beneficial when categorising tasks according to their importance and urgency. When we know which activities are essential and urgent, we can redirect our focus away from unimportant and non-urgent tasks.

Self-Care

Self-care isn't just a trendy term; it's a fundamental pillar of overall well-being. Contrary to the notion that self-care is indulgent or selfish, it's a prerequisite for being an effective and emotionally available parent. When you prioritise self-care, you're refuelling your energy and setting a powerful example for your children. My biggest motto in life is " We have to take care of ourselves to take care of those around you" We can never pour from an empty cup.

1. Delegate and Seek Support. Remember, you don't have to do it all alone. Feel free to delegate tasks or ask for help. Seek support from family, friends, or even professional services if needed. A strong support network can free up self-care time without compromising parental responsibilities.

2. Engage in mindful self-care activities that rejuvenate your body, mind, and spirit. Whether practising yoga, going for a body massage, indulging in a soothing bath, reading a book, or pursuing a hobby, these moments of self-indulgence can enhance your well-being and provide a sense of balance.

3. Communicate Openly. Clear and open communication with your partner and children is paramount. Express your needs and boundaries honestly. This helps set realistic expectations and fosters an environment of mutual understanding and cooperation.

Mom Guilt is that nagging feeling of inadequacy or unease that arises when a parent believes they are falling short of expectations, whether those are societal norms, their ideals, or even comparisons to other parents. It's a universal emotion triggered by various factors, such as taking time for yourself, pursuing personal interests, or delegating childcare tasks.

The first step in overcoming mom guilt is to acknowledge that it's a common experience shared by parents across the spectrum. It doesn't necessarily reflect your parenting abilities but rather the internal struggle balancing responsibilities and personal needs. By normalising these feelings, you can begin to address them more effectively.

Embracing self-compassion is a powerful tool in combating mom guilt. Treat yourself with the same kindness and understanding that you offer to others.

Remember, taking care of yourself doesn't make you a less devoted parent—it enables you to be more present and patient with your children.

Reevaluate your definition of a "good parent." It's essential to realise that being the best parent doesn't mean sacrificing every ounce of your well-being. By practising self-care, you're enriching your life and showing your children the importance of valuing oneself.

Remember that it's not about the quantity of time you spend with your children but the quality of that time. Engage in activities that create meaningful connections and memories. When you take time for yourself, you're allowing yourself to recharge, ensuring that your time with your children is more fulfilling and energetic.

Just as you teach your children life skills, you also model emotional well-being. By confronting mom's guilt head-on, you demonstrate the importance of self-awareness, self-care, and resilience. This valuable lesson will serve them as they navigate their journeys in the future.

Mom guilt is just one thread in the grand tapestry of parenting and self-care. Viewing it as an opportunity for growth rather than a roadblock is essential. You can gradually transform guilt into empowerment by practising self-compassion, embracing open dialogue, and redefining your priorities. Remember, a balanced parent is a happier and more fulfilled parent.

The phrase "happy wife, happy life" is often used colloquially to imply that a wife's happiness is crucial to the overall well-being and harmony of a household. When one partner is happy, especially in a traditional family structure where the wife often manages the household's emotional climate, it can positively influence the overall mood and functioning of the family. The happiness of both partners in a marriage is vital. While the phrase might be simplistic, it does remind us that in any relationship, the happiness of each matters. A fulfilling and harmonious life together stems from mutual happiness, understanding, and shared responsibilities.

Your journey as a full-time mother need not be at the expense of your personal growth. By leveraging AI, you can find new ways to learn, enhance your well-being, connect with others, and balance your aspirations and responsibilities. As we progress, we'll explore how AI can play a role in your financial management and entrepreneurial endeavours.

Chapter 5: Managing Finances with AI

Financial management is critical to running a household and planning for the future. This chapter explores how AI can assist full-time mothers in budgeting, investing, and teaching financial literacy to their children.

5.1. AI in Personal Finance Management

Several AI-powered personalised budgeting tools have gained popularity among moms and general users due to their effectiveness in managing personal finances. Optimal AI finance applications deliver sophisticated functionalities, including customising budgets tailored to individual needs, projecting upcoming financial tendencies, and streamlining crucial financial operations automatically. These applications should also provide an intuitive user interface, ensure the highest level of security, and maintain clear and straightforward pricing.

Are you seeking assistance creating a budget, managing investments, or planning retirement? Once you've determined your financial priorities, you can seek out apps specialising in those fields. Then, evaluate them based on their features, use of AI for personalisation, security measures, cost transparency, and user experience.

Ensuring that any finance app you use specialising security measures is essential. Look for password protection, 256-bit encryption authentication, and up-to-date algorithms and privacy practices. Furthermore, the application should communicate its data handling policies. It should only sell your information to third parties with your knowledge. Here are some of the most popular ones:

Cleo: Cleo is a free AI budget app which can transform your financial mindset. It functions like a virtual financial consultant, offering immediate notifications, advice, and visual aids to keep you aware and in control of your spending patterns. When you connect your bank to Cleo, it can securely analyse your transaction data. Cleo takes a look at your banking activity – identifying trends and habits. This approach can contribute to interrupting impulsive spending behaviours and diminishing financial stress. It instantly answers your queries using NLP, making the app feel like a trusted friend guiding you through your financial endeavours. Its recommendations become even more tailored to your spending habits over time.

Eva Money: Regarding investment management, Eva Money is at the forefront. This AI-driven app offers a comprehensive platform for individuals looking to optimise their investment portfolios. Eva Money utilises advanced algorithms to assess market trends, analyse risk factors, and suggest suitable investment opportunities tailored to your financial goals. Eva Money, even novice investors can make decisions with confidence. The app provides personalised recommendations, real-time performance tracking, and detailed reports to keep you updated on your investments. Furthermore, Eva Money's intuitive interface and user-friendly features make it personalised to users of all experience levels.

MintZip: If you're looking for an AI money management app that excels in budgeting, MintZip is an excellent choice. MintZip combines cutting-edge AI technology with robust budgeting tools to empower users to manage their expenses effectively. By categorising transactions, tracking spending patterns, and providing actionable insights, MintZip helps you stay on top of your budget effortlessly. One of the standout features of MintZip is its ability to categorise potential areas for cost-cutting. The app can suggest practical ways to save money and optimise your budget by analysing your expenses. Moreover, MintZip provides personalised notifications and reminders to ensure you never miss a bill payment or exceed your set spending limits.

PocketGuard: PocketGuard uses AI to analyse your spending habits and income, helping you to stay on top of bills, budget for future expenses, and identify opportunities to save money.

WallyGPT: WallyGPT uses AI to give you insights into analysing spending behaviour, helping you set and achieve your financial goals by tracking income and expenses and offering a savings target.

Olivia.ai: Olivia.ai is an AI money management app with intelligent financial advice and personalised guidance. By analysing your financial data, Olivia.ai can offer tailored recommendations to help you make intelligent financial decisions. Whether you need assistance with investments, debt, or personalised savings, Olivia.ai has you covered.

These budgeting tools, powered by AI, are handy for busy moms who need to manage household budgets efficiently. They offer a user-friendly way to get a clear picture of financial health, track spending, and plan for future financial goals. By leveraging the power of AI, these apps have empowered individuals to take control of their finances with confidence and ease. With the rapid advancement of technology, these AI money management apps are set to further revolutionise how we handle our money. Embrace the future of personal finance by exploring these remarkable platforms and harnessing their potential to achieve your financial goals.

5.2. Teaching Financial Literacy to Children

5.2.1. How to Teach Your Child About Money?

Many parents feel uncomfortable talking to their children about money, and teaching financial education at school or college is not compulsory. The good news is plenty of interactive money-related resources are available to our children from 3 to 18 years old.

Introducing financial literacy early in life aids children in establishing enduring, positive financial behaviours. The main principles of financial literacy include earning, saving, investing, protecting, spending, and borrowing.

Younger individuals are often more susceptible to the influences of social media and marketing tactics that promote consumerism. Financial literacy can encourage habits that help children avoid debt traps later in life. Children can form money habits starting as young as age 5. Individuals generally make more informed financial choices when thoroughly understanding money management principles. Studies have consistently demonstrated that instilling money management skills in children early on is beneficial, as it fosters financial knowledge and habits throughout their lives. In an ideal world, parents would initiate conversations about money with their children at a very young age. There are many ways to get our children to think about money. We can help children understand how household finances work by engaging them in our finances. Whether it's a grocery shopping trip or paying the bills, we can walk children through our decisions. We can also let kids listen to our conversations with accountants and other financial professionals.

In today's digital age, video games have become more than just a source of entertainment for kids; they can also serve as valuable tools for teaching money management skills and finances.

The central idea is that certain video games incorporate financial elements, such as budgeting, saving, and investing, into their gameplay. These games provide an interactive experience in which players engage in financial decision-making and observe the outcomes of their actions. Navigating virtual economies teaches players about earning and managing money in a safe and engaging environment.

Using video games as educational tools has benefits, such as making financial learning fun and relatable for kids.

Ultimately, the goal is to empower young individuals with the knowledge and skills necessary to make informed financial decisions in the real world. Video games can play a role in achieving this objective by turning financial education into an interactive and enjoyable experience for children.

Despite the perception that video games don't impart significant life skills to children, there is, in fact, a substantial opportunity for them to gain knowledge about financial matters through gaming.

Parents need to be actively involved in discussing the financial elements of video games with their children to highlight and enhance the learning of these lessons. In this way, young individuals can learn about establishing savings objectives, cultivating healthy spending practices, and creating and adhering to a budget. These lessons remain valuable and applicable beyond when the video game is substituted with other interests.

Paying an allowance can be an effective way to help your child learn good financial habits. Instead of directly purchasing toys for our children, parents can use the traditional method of having the kids earn money through completing household chores. That way, they learn the connection between labour and income. Providing children with an allowance effectively instils positive money management habits from an early age. Children are often prepared to start receiving an allowance, learning about money, and saving around the time they begin kindergarten, typically at 5 or 6 years old. The decision to pay kids an allowance is different for every family. However, the majority of parents say it's essential for kids to understand the value of working for their money. The question is how do we set an allowance for our kids?

A frequently adopted guideline for giving an allowance is to pay children between £1 and £2 weekly for each year of their age. According to this guideline, an 8-year-old would earn an allowance of £8-£16 per week, whereas a 16-year-old would receive £16 to £32 weekly.

Alternatively, children can be paid based on each chore they complete weekly, assuming they must work to earn their allowance.

Parents can decide on a set payment for chores like washing the car, cleaning windows, mowing the lawn, doing the dishes, vacuuming, assisting with laundry, walking the dog, and tidying up their room.

Parents might also adopt a goal-oriented strategy to establish the appropriate amount for an allowance. Consider, for instance, if your child aims to save £500 to purchase a gaming system. You can assist them in breaking down their goal to provide a clearer perspective on how much they need to earn. They must make around £42 per month, £10 per week and £1.4 per day.

Visualising the numbers can aid children in determining the feasibility of their goal and understanding the steps necessary to achieve it. Acquiring the skill of goal-setting in this manner is a valuable asset for managing their finances effectively as adults.

A key advantage of providing children with an allowance is that it offers them direct experience in earning and managing money. Providing children with an allowance can nurture their financial skills, empowering them to make more informed money decisions in adulthood. Additionally, it fosters economic self-reliance, reducing their dependence on parents for monetary needs. When children have money to manage, they can learn budgeting skills and understand the significance of saving. Implementing a system where chores are compensated can instil a sense of responsibility in children and teach them the worth of earning money through work. Of course, we can also reward them with other things like screen time or taking them to their favourite restaurants.

Where does our money come from?

For younger children(ages 9 and younger), Mom and Dad might have an endless supply of money. Eventually, they will become curious about the source of your money. This presents a chance to discuss how you earn a specific amount monthly for the work you perform at your job. If your young children have seen you taking money out of an ATM, they might easily imagine it as a magical device dispensing unlimited cash. If only it were that simple.

For younger children, the concept of a limit to your money supply may become apparent and intuitive. Hence, during your next trip to the bank or an ATM, it would be beneficial to highlight that your account carries a limited amount of money, which decreases each time you withdraw cash. Piggy Bank can be a helpful reference point. If you start with £10 in it, you can take out £1 per day, but you'll have less money in the bank each time. By day ten, their piggy bank will be empty.

How much money do we have?

Kids naturally begin to observe their possessions (or lack thereof), often triggered by seeing things like a friend being driven in an ultra-luxurious car or hearing about a lavish island holiday their friend recently enjoyed. This naturally progresses to inquiries about how your financial situation stacks up against other families. You don't have to give your kids the exact amount you make yearly. These inquiries can be an opportunity to reassure your children and manage their expectations regarding spending on toys and other non-essential items.

Preteens (Ages 10 to 12)

What determines the price of various things?

Kids will notice that a pack of pens costs around £3, but a 4K television will set you back £300. So, who precisely sets these prices?

Explaining this phenomenon requires delving into the fundamental principles of supply and demand. It is a great idea to use video games as an example. Ask them why the latest edition of a popular PS5 game might cost £60, whereas the older version can be had for £30. Their first answer would usually be that players want the latest one more. Aware of this desire for the newest edition, companies selling these games tend to charge more for the latest release in pursuit of profit. This is the demand at work. Likewise, the amount of a particular item that's available—the supply—will have much to do with how much you pay. If you purchase the final copy of a sought-after video game from a store, you could sell it outside for a price higher than what you paid. My son was purchasing Prime drinks online and then reselling them at a profit when there used to be a massive demand for them. That was an excellent example to illustrate fundamental economic principles like supply and demand and the concept of buying low and selling high. This hands-on experience is invaluable in teaching financial literacy and business acumen.

So what about that £3 pack of pens and the expensive TV? The market is flooded with pens from numerous manufacturers, and people generally aren't inclined to pay a high price for a standard ballpoint pen. TVs cost more, so fewer are on the market, and customers are willing to pay for the perfect ones.

Teenagers (Ages 13 to 19)

How do stocks work?

Once your children reach secondary school, they will likely have heard stories about certain company stocks either soaring to great heights in value or plummeting dramatically after a rapid ascent.

Start by explaining that a stock is a small piece of a company. Owning a stock means you own a tiny part of that company, just like owning a piece of a puzzle. Explain that stocks are bought and sold on the stock market, like a big online store for buying and selling company parts. People buy stocks hoping the company will do well and the stock will be worth more later. They can then sell the stock for more than they paid for it. Make it clear that the value of stocks can go up and down. If the company is doing well, more people might want to buy the stock, and the price increases. If the company is not doing well, the price might go down. Investing in stocks can be risky – they could lose money if the stock value decreases. But there is also a chance to make money if the value increases. Finally, mention that many people buy stocks as a long-term investment. They keep the stocks for years, hoping they will grow in value over time, even if they go up and down in the short term. Several apps use AI and virtual simulations to allow users to trade shares with virtual money. These platforms are designed to provide a realistic experience of the stock market without the financial risk of real trading. Some popular ones include Investopedia Stock Simulator, Wall Street Survivor and Stock Trainer.

Here are some family-oriented apps designed to help teach children about money management and financial responsibility.

1. Savings Spree

Savings Spree is a fun and addictive game app which teaches young kids (age 5-11) smart financial habits. Money lessons are taught through games and they aim to encourage kids to save money. It is a great choice for parents who would like to give their kids a head start on their knowledge on financial literacy.

2. World of Money

World of Money offers video lessons and interactive content on various financial topics tailored for youth aged 7-21. The lessons for younger users cover more basic topics, such as the difference between needs and wants. Lessons for older users are more advanced and cover topics like budgeting and how credit cards work. Tools like quizzes and flashcards make learning about finances engaging and effective for children. Many lessons are available, covering just about all the major financial topics. They offer 3-4 minute-long bite-sized videos; our kids can learn financial literacy by using this app for just five minutes daily. The World of Money app is 100% free to download and has no subscription fee. It is a great choice for anyone with a tight budget who wants to learn more about money.

3. BusyKid

BusyKid is a chore and allowance app that allows parents to assign tasks and pay allowances upon completion. The app aims to teach children about the value of hard work and the basics of personal finance. Children can earn a weekly allowance based on the chores they complete.

The app enables children to divide their earnings into savings, spending, and sharing (donating to charity). It offers options for children to invest in real stocks, learn about investing, and grow their savings. BusyKid also provides a prepaid card for kids, allowing them to purchase with the money they've earned under parental supervision.

4. Greenlight

It is a debit card for kids managed by parents. It aims to teach children how to manage money through real-life experience while giving parents control and oversight. Parents can load money onto the Greenlight card as an allowance or for specific chores. The app includes features for setting spending limits and store-specific controls. It allows parents to oversee transactions and monitor balances. Greenlight also offers educational content to teach children about saving, spending, earning, and investing. The app provides savings goals and interest options to encourage children to save money.

5. FamZoo

FamZoo is a family-friendly app that offers prepaid cards and a financial education platform for kids and teens. It provides prepaid cards for each family member, allowing parents to transfer money to their children.

Includes features for tracking spending, saving, and setting financial goals. Offers a virtual family bank to simulate real-world banking experiences.

6. GoHenry

GoHenry is a money management tool with a prepaid debit card and an app with parental controls, designed for children aged 6 to 18. Customisable prepaid debit card for kids. Parents can set spending limits and monitor transactions. Features to encourage saving and charitable giving.

7. Bankaroo

Bankaroo is a virtual bank designed to teach younger kids about money management. A virtual savings tracker that helps kids manage their allowances, gifts, and chore money. Educational content that teaches basic money concepts. Available in multiple languages and offers a school program.

8. RoosterMoney

RoosterMoney is an allowance and chore management app that helps children learn about saving, spending, and giving. Track allowances, set chores, and save towards goals. Parents can manage the child's account, adding or removing funds as necessary. Offers a spend-save-give model to teach kids about different aspects of financial responsibility.

Whether or not to pay your children an allowance is personal, and there are different reasons for doing so. If you choose to pay one, offering your kids some guidance on how to use it is helpful. This encompasses the importance of allocating a portion of their income to savings before making any expenditures and teaching them the value of donating some of their money to charity. The more frequently you engage in discussions about money with children, the better equipped they will be with the necessary knowledge to handle their financial management when it arises.

There are a few innovative education platforms that offer a variety of engaging online courses. Some great examples include Hands-on Banking, Juni and Outschool.

They offer resources to help individuals learn more about money management. Their programmes include a variety of tools and information designed to educate users on various aspects of financial literacy, from basic money management principles to more complex financial topics.

5.2.2. How to Teach Your Child About Cryptocurrency?

As digital currencies become more prevalent in today's economy, understanding cryptocurrencies can give children a more comprehensive view of the modern financial landscape. This knowledge equips them to better understand various aspects of finance, including digital transactions, the concept of decentralised finance, and the evolving nature of money and investments. It's an essential addition to traditional financial literacy topics like saving, budgeting, and understanding credit.

Your child might be aware of cryptocurrency and Bitcoin, perhaps having seen eye-catching videos on TikTok or talked about it with friends. Yet, they may need help understanding the importance of these concepts. Some might be knowledgeable about these terms and eager to purchase electronics using crypto or invest in digital currencies. Or, they might have no interest at all in cryptocurrencies.

Regardless of their interest level, as a fundamental aspect of responsible parenting, it's our duty to aid our children in comprehending the complexities of the financial world. With younger individuals now incorporating cryptocurrency into their plans for retirement investment, understanding cryptocurrency may be significant for children.

5.3. What is Cryptocurrency?

Digital Currency for a New Era

Cryptocurrency is a groundbreaking form of money designed for the digital era. It exists solely in the digital realm, representing a shift from traditional, tangible forms of currency to an entirely virtual format. Unlike conventional currencies, it exists only in digital form - no physical coins or notes. Cryptocurrencies are composed of complex code, created and stored electronically, using cryptographic principles to secure transactions.

Core Characteristics of Cryptocurrencies

Cryptocurrency is a unique type of digital money that exists only on computers and the internet, protected by very complex secret codes to keep it safe. Unlike regular money, it doesn't need banks to move it around because it uses a special network of computers for that. It's kept in a unique app called a digital wallet, and you can use it to buy things online and sometimes in stores. One exciting thing about cryptocurrency is its value can change quickly like a rollercoaster. It's a new, cool kind of money made for our modern digital world!

Blockchain Technology: The Backbone of Cryptocurrency

Defining Blockchain Technology

Blockchain is a digital ledger, a continuously growing list of records called blocks, which are linked using cryptography. Let me try to make this easier to understand by moms and kids who are just starting to learn about cryptocurrency. Imagine blockchain technology as a magical diary that everyone in a large group shares.

This diary is very special and works differently than any diary you might have at home.

1. The Shared Magical Diary: This diary doesn't belong to just one person. Instead, everyone in the group has their own copy. Whenever something new is written in one diary, it magically appears in all the other diaries too.

2. Writing in the Diary: Let's say someone wants to send a digital sticker to a friend. When they do this, it's like writing a note in the diary. This note says who sent the sticker, who received it, and which sticker it was.

3. Checking the Notes: Before a note becomes part of the diary, the group makes sure it's truthful. Some special members of the group, like detectives, look at the note to check that everything is correct and that the sticker really belongs to the person sending it.

4. Adding Pages: Once a lot of notes have been checked and approved, they get put together on a new page in the diary. Each new page is attached to the last page, making a chain of pages. That's why it's called a 'blockchain' – it's a chain of pages (or blocks) in the diary.

5. Magic Ink: The diary uses a special magic ink that never fades and can't be erased. Once something is written with this ink, it stays there forever. This makes sure that no one can change what was written and everything stays honest.

6. Everyone's Diary is the Same: The magic of this diary is that when a new page is added in one diary, it appears in all the diaries at the same time. This means everyone always has the exact same diary, with all the same notes.

7. Looking at the Diary: Anyone can look at the pages of this diary, but the names of people are written in a secret code. You can see all the notes and stickers being sent, but you can't easily see who is sending them.

8. Why It's Special: This magical diary is important because it helps everyone trust each other. It makes sure that when someone says they sent a sticker, they really did. And since nobody can change what's written, everyone knows the diary is always telling the truth.

Blockchain is like this magical diary. It helps people exchange things like digital money or information in a way that is safe, honest, and easy for everyone to check. It's a new and exciting way of sharing and keeping track of information in our digital world!

Security and Transparency of Blockchain

Security: The Super-Secure Diary

1. Unbreakable Locks: Think of blockchain as a super-secure diary that uses strong locks. These locks are special codes (cryptography) so complex that they're nearly impossible to break. It's like having a diary with a lock that only you know the combination to, but even stronger.

2. Chain of Pages: Each page (block) in this diary has a copy of the last page's lock, and it adds its own new lock, too. If someone tries to change something on one page, they would have to change the locks on all the pages that come after it, which is really hard. That's how blockchain keeps all its information safe.

3. Many Copies: This isn't just one diary – it's like every person in your class had the same diary. So, if someone changed something in their diary, everyone would know because their diary would differ from all the others. This means it's hard for anyone to cheat or change what's been written.

Transparency: The Glass House

1. See-Through Walls: Now, imagine a house made of glass where you can see everything inside. Blockchain is like that. Everyone can see all the transactions (like people trading digital stickers). Still, they can't see the names of the people making the trades. They can see what's happening, but who is doing it? It needs to be corrected.

2. Public Ledger: The information on the blockchain is like having a public bulletin board in the middle of town where everyone can read the notices. But instead of names, there are special codes that represent people. This ensures that personal details stay private while everyone knows what's happening.

3. Trustworthy System: Because everyone can see the transactions and it's hard to change them without anyone noticing, blockchain is reliable. It's like having a community where everyone helps keep an eye on things to ensure everything is fair and honest.

So, blockchain is like a super-secure diary with unbreakable locks and transparent glass walls. It keeps all the information about trades and transactions safe and lets everyone see what's happening without revealing personal details. This combination of security and transparency makes blockchain a reliable and secure way to handle digital transactions!

Utilisation and Exchange of Cryptocurrencies

1. Digital Spending Money: Cryptocurrencies are digital tokens or points you can use to buy things. Just like you might use coins in a video game to get new outfits for your character, you can use cryptocurrencies to purchase real things online, like games, toys, or even services.

2. Digital Wallet - Your Online Piggy Bank: You need a digital wallet to use cryptocurrencies. This is like a piggy bank or a particular folder on your computer or phone where you keep your digital tokens. You can see how many tokens you have, send some to others, or receive more.

3. Trading Cryptocurrencies - Swapping Digital Stickers: Imagine you have a digital sticker that's really popular, and your friend has a different sticker you want. You can swap stickers using your digital wallets. This is like exchanging cryptocurrencies. You can trade different types of digital tokens with people worldwide.

4. Shopping with Cryptocurrencies: Some online stores and even some physical shops let you buy things using cryptocurrencies. It's just like shopping with regular money, but you use your digital wallet to pay. You choose the cryptocurrency option at checkout, and the store tells you how many digital tokens you need to pay.

5. Value Changes - The Fluctuating Lemonade Stand Prices: The value of cryptocurrencies can go up and down, like if you were running a lemonade stand and changing your lemonade's price every day. Some days, people might pay more digital tokens for the same glass of lemonade, while others might pay less. This is because the value of cryptocurrencies changes based on how many people want to buy them and how many are available.

6. Exchanging for Real Money: You can exchange cryptocurrencies for regular money, like dollars or euros. This is similar to exchanging foreign money at the airport when you return from a vacation. There are special online places where you can swap your digital tokens for real money, which then gets added to your regular bank account.

7. Earning Cryptocurrencies - Digital Allowance: Sometimes, you can earn cryptocurrencies by doing specific tasks online, like filling out surveys, playing games, or learning about new digital tokens. It's like getting an allowance, but instead of getting cash, you get digital tokens in your digital wallet.

Real-World Applications of Blockchain Technology

1. Trading Cards in a Digital Album (NFTs): Just like kids collect and trade unique cards or stickers, blockchain technology can collect digital versions of these things, called NFTs (Non-Fungible Tokens). Each NFT is unique, like a one-of-a-kind sticker, and you can buy, sell, or trade them online. They could be anything digital, like artwork, music, or even a tweet!

2. Super Safe Health Records: Imagine if your health records were kept in a unique book that only certain doctors and nurses could look at when they needed to. Blockchain can keep medical records safe and private, ensuring only the people you give permission to can see them. It's like having a secret diary for your health information.

3. A Fair Voting System: Voting in elections could be like a class vote on what game to play during recess. Blockchain can ensure everyone's vote is counted and no one can cheat, like ensuring each child gets only one vote for the game and that all votes are counted correctly.

4. Tracking Items from Start to Finish (Supply Chain): Imagine following the journey of a chocolate bar from where the cocoa beans are grown to when they're in your hand. Blockchain can track items like food, clothes, and toys from the start of their journey to the end. This helps make sure they're made safely and fairly.

5. Smart Contracts – Automatic Agreements: These are like automatic promises. If you do your chores, then you automatically get your allowance. Smart contracts on blockchain work the same way. When someone does what they agreed to, the blockchain automatically does its part, like paying them. This could be used for renting houses, buying music, and more.

6. Making Games More Fun (Gaming): In some video games, you can earn items or characters to keep or trade. Blockchain ensures that the items

you earn or buy in games belong to you and can't be copied, making the gaming experience even more exciting.

7. Protecting the Environment: Blockchain can be used to track how products impact the environment. For example, it can track how much energy is used to make a product, helping companies be more eco-friendly.

Blockchain technology is like a magic book or a super-computer that can be used for many things beyond digital money. From keeping our health records safe and making voting fairer to tracking our food and making games more fun, it's a powerful tool that can help make our world safer, more equitable, and more enjoyable!

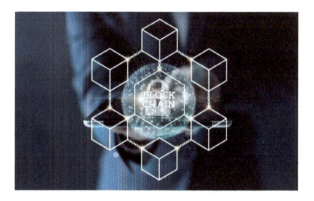

Types of Cryptocurrencies

1. Bitcoin - The First and Most Famous: Think of Bitcoin as the first ever magical digital coin. It was the first cryptocurrency ever made, like the first telephone. It's the most well-known, and many people like to use it to buy things online or as an investment, like digital gold.

2. Ethereum - More Than Just Money: Ethereum is like a magical coin, a wizard! Apart from being used like money, Ethereum can also make agreements called 'smart contracts.' These are promises that automatically happen when certain conditions are met, like automatically getting a reward for finishing a puzzle.

3. Ripple (XRP) - The Fast Money Messenger: Ripple is like a super-fast digital postal service for money. It's designed to send money (like digital

coins) worldwide quickly and with low fees. It's perfect for banks and financial institutions to move large amounts of money around the globe.

4. Litecoin - Bitcoin's Little Brother: Litecoin is much like Bitcoin, but it's like the younger sibling. It's designed to do many of the same things but faster. It's like if Bitcoin is a mail truck, then Litecoin is a speedy delivery scooter.

5. Cardano - The Eco-friendly Coin: Imagine a digital coin that's also good for the environment. That's Cardano. It's designed to do things similar to Ethereum but uses much less energy, making it more eco-friendly. It's like riding a bicycle instead of a car to help reduce pollution.

6. Polkadot - Connecting Different Blockchains: Polkadot is like a magical bridge connecting different islands, each island being a separate blockchain. It lets different blockchains talk to each other and work together. It's like having a translator who can speak many languages, helping everyone to understand each other.

7. Stablecoins - The Steady Coins: Stablecoins are like digital coins with training wheels. They are designed to have a stable value, not going up and down a lot like other cryptocurrencies. They're usually tied to the value of something sturdy, like a country's money (like the dollar) or gold.

The Value of Cryptocurrencies and Investment Perspective

1. Digital Treasure Coins: Think of cryptocurrencies like digital treasure coins. Just like treasures, their value can be exciting. Sometimes, these digital coins can become more valuable, like a rare toy everyone wants to buy. Other times, they might be less valuable, depending on how many people like them and how many are available.

2. A Roller Coaster of Value: The value of cryptocurrencies can go up and down, just like a roller coaster ride. One day, your digital coins might buy many things, and another, they might buy less. This is because their value changes based on how popular they are and what people are willing to pay for them.

3. Saving for the Future (Investing): Some people like to collect these digital coins, hoping they will be worth more. This is like saving up your unique toys or cards, thinking they might be worth much more when you're older. But just like with toys, there's no guarantee they will be worth more. It's a guessing game.

4. A Digital Piggy Bank (Cryptocurrency Wallet): To keep these digital coins, you use a digital wallet, which is like a piggy bank but for your digital treasure. You can add more coins to it or take some out to exchange for regular money.

5. Being Careful with Your Digital Coins: Like any treasure, you must be careful. The value can change quickly, and you can lose what you've put in. It's important not to put all your treasures in one place and to only use what you can afford to be without, especially for things like saving for a rainy day or your future.

6. Learning and Watching: Before collecting these digital coins, it's a good idea to learn as much as you can about them. Watching how their value changes can be exciting and help you understand how this digital treasure works.

Cryptocurrencies are like digital treasures with a value that can go up and down. Some people collect them as an investment, hoping they'll be worth more. But just like any investment, it's essential to be careful and not use the money you need for other important things. It's a new and exciting world, but you must be intelligent and cautious, just like any adventure with treasures!

Earning and Using Cryptocurrency: A Guide for Moms

Earning Cryptocurrency:

- Freelancing or Remote Work: Many online platforms now offer payment in cryptocurrencies for freelance work. Suppose you have skills in writing, graphic design, web development, or any other area. In that case, you can earn cryptocurrency by providing these services.

- Cryptocurrency Mining: While more technical, cryptocurrency mining involves using computer power to solve complex mathematical problems and maintain the blockchain. Successful miners earn cryptocurrency as a reward. However, it requires significant technical knowledge and computer resources.

- Participating in Airdrops: Occasionally, new cryptocurrencies will distribute free tokens in a process known as an 'airdrop' to promote their launch. Observing cryptocurrency forums and news can alert you to these opportunities.

Using Cryptocurrency:

- Shopping Online: More and more retailers are accepting cryptocurrencies as payment for goods and services. You can use your digital currency to purchase everyday items from online marketplaces to specific brand stores.

    - Investing: Cryptocurrency can be a long-term investment. While it carries risk due to price volatility, many people buy and hold cryptocurrencies, hoping their value will increase.

    - Trading: For those who understand the market well, trading cryptocurrencies on exchanges can be a way to earn profits. However, this is risky and requires a good understanding of the market dynamics.

    - Paying Bills: Some services allow you to pay your regular bills with cryptocurrencies by converting them into your local currency when making payments.

Learning and Staying Informed:

    - Educational Resources: Many free resources are available online to learn about cryptocurrencies, from introductory guides to in-depth technical explanations.

    - Community Engagement: Joining cryptocurrency forums and community groups can provide support, updates, and advice from more experienced individuals in the field.

For moms interested in digital currencies, there are various ways to earn and use cryptocurrency. It's an exciting and evolving field, offering financial involvement and learning opportunities. However, as with any monetary endeavour, it's essential to conduct thorough research, understand the risks involved, and proceed cautiously. With the right approach, cryptocurrency can be both a rewarding learning experience and a novel way to manage finances in the digital age.

The Future of Blockchain

As we look towards the future, blockchain technology is poised to significantly transform our daily lives in particularly relevant ways for moms. Picture a world where managing household tasks, personal finances, and your family's health records is streamlined and secure, thanks to blockchain.

This technology, best known for powering cryptocurrencies, is much more than digital money. It's a secure system for recording information – a system that's almost impossible to hack or cheat. In the coming years, blockchain could revolutionise how we handle everyday tasks. For instance, keeping track of medical records could be a breeze; you'll have all your family's health information securely stored and easily accessible without the fear of this sensitive data being compromised.

Imagine shopping with complete confidence about the origin and safety of products, whether food or toys, as blockchain's tracking capabilities provide transparent and reliable information about their journey from production to your home.

Financially, managing savings and making payments could become more straightforward and safer. Sending money to a relative across the globe could be as easy and cost-effective as sending a text message.

For your children, blockchain could offer interactive and secure ways to learn about money management and savings, setting a foundation for responsible financial habits.

In essence, the evolution of blockchain promises to make many aspects of life more organised, secure, and transparent, providing moms with more time, peace of mind, and confidence in the safety and authenticity of the products and services they rely on. As this technology continues to evolve, it has the potential to simplify, secure, and enrich family life in numerous ways.

5.4. AI for Smart Shopping and Deals

AI (Artificial Intelligence) is revolutionising the shopping experience, making it more accessible, efficient, and often more cost-effective – especially beneficial for busy moms. Here's how AI is shaping smart shopping and finding deals:

AI for Smart Shopping

Personalised Shopping Experience

Several AI-powered apps can help moms with personalised shopping experiences, making finding products tailored to their preferences and needs easier. Think of it as having a personal shopping assistant who knows exactly what you like, saving you time in finding the right products.

Here are some notable ones:

Amazon: Amazon's AI algorithms analyse your browsing and purchase history to recommend products that fit your preferences. This can be incredibly helpful for quickly finding items that match your interests.

Stitch Fix: This app uses AI to provide a personal styling service. Based on your sizes, and budget and style preferences. Stitch Fix's AI stylist selects clothing and accessories for you, which are then sent to your home for trying on.

Honey: While primarily known for finding and applying coupon codes at checkout, Honey also offers a Droplist feature, which tracks price drops on items you're interested in, helping you purchase at the best time.

Pinterest: Although not a shopping app per se, Pinterest uses AI to tailor its feed to your interests. It can be a great source of inspiration for products, from home decor to clothing, and often includes links to purchase items.

The Yes: This app is a personal shopping assistant that learns your style as you shop. The app refines its understanding of your preferences by giving feedback on different products to improve product recommendations.

ShopSavvy: This app allows you to scan barcodes or search for items to compare prices across various retailers. Its AI helps find the best deals and even alerts you about price drops.

Chatbots on Retail Websites: Many e-commerce sites now have AI-powered chatbots to help you find products based on your questions and preferences. These virtual assistants can guide you through product selections and offer personalised recommendations.

Lyst: For fashion-focused moms, Lyst aggregates products from multiple online retailers and uses AI to recommend clothing and accessories based on your past searches and purchases.

These AI apps and tools can significantly streamline the shopping process, offering personalised recommendations and deals that save time and money, particularly beneficial for busy moms.

Price Comparison and Best Deals

AI algorithms can scan the internet to compare prices across retailers. You can get the best deal available without manually checking multiple websites.

Here are some of the more popular platforms:

Honey: This browser extension automatically searches for and applies coupon codes at checkout. Honey also has a feature that tracks price changes on specific items and notifies you when the price drops.

CamelCamelCamel: Mainly for Amazon shoppers, this tool tracks the price history of items and alerts you when prices drop. It's great for spotting the best times to buy.

Google Shopping: Google's AI-driven comparison tool allows you to search for products and see prices from various sellers. It helps find the best deals and includes reviews to help you make informed decisions.

Price.com: This app aggregates prices from different platforms, including traditional retailers and second-hand markets. Its AI technology helps you find the best deals across new, used, refurbished, and rental goods.

Rakuten (formerly Ebates): While primarily a cashback site, Rakuten also offers the ability to compare prices and find discounts and special offers across a wide range of retailers.

Paribus: This service tracks your online purchases and requests refunds on your behalf if a price drops or if there's a late delivery. It integrates with your email to monitor receipts and purchases.

Pricena: For moms in the Middle East, Pricena is a price comparison website that can help busy moms compare the prices of a wide range of products from various online stores in countries like UAE, Saudi Arabia, Egypt, and others.

Flipp: This app aggregates weekly ads, coupons, and deals from over 2000 retailers. You can quickly search for specific items or browse deals by category.

Using these AI-driven tools, moms can easily compare prices, get alerts on price drops, and find the best deals, making their shopping more budget-friendly and efficient.

Virtual Try-Ons and Previews

AI-powered virtual try-on and preview apps have become increasingly popular, especially for shopping for clothing and accessories. These apps use augmented reality (AR) and AI to provide a realistic visualisation of how products would look to the user. Here are some apps that can help moms with virtual try-ons and previews:

Zara: The Zara app offers an AR experience where you can see models wearing different outfits as if they are in front of you. You can rotate the view to see the outfit from various angles, providing a more comprehensive idea of how it looks.

ASOS: The ASOS app includes a feature called 'See My Fit,' which allows you to see what a particular item of clothing would look like on different body types, helping you gauge how it might look.

Sephora Virtual Artist: While not for clothing, the Sephora Virtual Artist app is perfect for trying on makeup products. You can try different shades of makeup virtually, seeing how they look on your face before purchasing.

IKEA Place: For home accessories and furniture, IKEA Place lets you virtually place furniture in your home. You can see how different items would fit and look in your space, which is extremely helpful for home decor decisions.

Warby Parker: Their app provides a virtual try-on for glasses. You can see how different frames look on your face through your phone's camera, making choosing the right pair of glasses easier.

L'Oréal Paris Virtual Try-On: Similar to Sephora, L'Oréal's app lets you try on various beauty products, including hair colours, to see how they would look on you.

Snapchat: Various brands partner with Snapchat to offer virtual try-ons through AR lenses. You can try on accessories like hats, sunglasses, and even some clothing items.

Amazon AR View: While primarily for home goods and electronics, Amazon's AR View feature helps visualise how products will look in your home, which can help select home accessories.

Gucci: Gucci's app offers an AR try-on feature for shoes. You can see how different styles of shoes would look on your feet, helping with the decision-making process.

These apps enhance the online shopping experience by reducing guesswork and helping to visualise products realistically. This technology makes shopping more fun and can lead to more satisfactory purchases with fewer returns.

In AI-enhanced shopping, voice-assisted shopping has emerged as a game-changer, especially for busy moms. Using voice commands with AI assistants like Amazon's Alexa or Google Assistant, you can effortlessly add items to your shopping list, reorder staples, or even make purchases without lifting a finger. Additionally, AI apps provide:

- Invaluable inventory updates and alerts.

- Notifying you when a coveted item is back in stock or has dropped in price.

- Ensuring you never miss out on a deal or necessity.

AI has revolutionised how we approach our weekly food schedules for meal planning and grocery shopping. Apps can suggest recipes based on dietary preferences, generate shopping lists, and even order groceries directly, streamlining the process. Furthermore, the checkout experience in online shopping has been significantly enhanced by AI, offering features like saved payment information and auto-filled shipping details, leading to a quicker and more seamless transaction process. Collectively, these AI-driven features not only save precious time but also elevate the efficiency and convenience of the shopping experience.

Chapter 6: Starting a Home-Based Business with AI

Entrepreneurship and AI: A Powerful Combination for Full-Time Mothers

Embarking on an entrepreneurial journey can be exciting and challenging, especially for full-time mothers. AI can play a crucial role in this endeavour, from the inception of a business idea to its execution and growth. This chapter focuses on leveraging AI to start and grow a home-based business.

6.1. Identifying Business Opportunities with AI

Identifying Business Opportunities with AI

In an age where Artificial Intelligence (AI) is reshaping industries, enterprising moms can leverage this technology to identify and develop innovative business ideas. AI's ability to analyse data, predict trends, and automate tasks can be instrumental in recognising and capitalising on business opportunities. Here's how moms can harness AI to become successful entrepreneurs.

Understanding AI and Its Capabilities

The first step is gaining a foundational understanding of AI. This involves familiarising yourself with basic AI concepts, how AI systems work, and their application in various industries. Online courses, webinars, and tech blogs are excellent resources for this learning journey. This knowledge helps envision how AI can solve real-world problems or enhance existing services and products.

Identifying Pain Points and Market Gaps

Observing daily challenges faced by families and communities can reveal potential business opportunities. AI can provide solutions to many of these challenges. For instance, AI could address issues in personalised education, efficient home management, or health and wellness tailored to individual needs. Analysing these pain points through the lens of AI's capabilities can inspire innovative business ideas.

Market Research and Analysis

Utilising AI tools for market research can provide deep insights into consumer behaviour, emerging trends, and competitor analysis. AI algorithms can process vast market data to identify unmet needs or upcoming trends. This information is crucial in validating the potential of a business idea and shaping it to meet market demands.

Leveraging AI for Business Planning

AI-powered tools can assist in developing robust business plans. They can help in financial modelling, market analysis, and risk assessment. AI can also provide predictive analytics to forecast market trends and business growth, aiding in strategic planning and decision-making.

Enhancing Customer Experience with AI

AI can be used to create personalised customer experiences, a key differentiator in today's market. From AI-driven recommendation systems to customer service chatbots, AI can enhance customer interaction and satisfaction, leading to higher retention and brand loyalty.

Networking and Collaboration

Engaging with AI communities, tech meetups, and online forums can provide valuable insights and collaboration opportunities. Networking with AI experts, tech entrepreneurs, and other business owners can offer guidance, mentorship, and potential partnerships.

Staying Agile and Adaptable

The AI landscape is continuously evolving. Staying updated with the most recent developments in AI technology and their implementation across various industries is crucial. This continuous educational journey guarantees that the business stays pertinent and flexible in response to evolving market trends.

Balancing Entrepreneurship with Motherhood

AI can also assist in balancing the demands of entrepreneurship with motherhood. AI-driven productivity tools, time management apps, and virtual assistants can help efficiently manage business tasks alongside family responsibilities.

For moms venturing into the entrepreneurial world, AI offers a pathway to innovative and successful business ideas. By understanding AI, identifying market needs, and leveraging AI for business planning and operations, mompreneurs can build enterprises that are not only profitable but also contribute to solving real-world problems. In harnessing the power of AI, moms can transform their unique perspectives and insights into viable business ventures, marking their place in the burgeoning landscape of AI-driven entrepreneurship.

6.2. AI in Business Planning and Management

AI in Business Planning and Management for Moms

In today's fast-paced world, where balancing family life with entrepreneurial ambitions can be challenging, Artificial Intelligence (AI) emerges as a powerful ally for moms in business planning and management. With its ability to process vast amounts of data and provide insights, AI can be a game-changer in several key areas.

Market Analysis and Consumer Insights

Utilising AI for market research offers an unparalleled advantage. AI algorithms can sift through massive datasets, analyse trends, and provide valuable insights into consumer behaviours and market dynamics. This is crucial for identifying niche markets or understanding gaps in the market that a business could fill. Moms can leverage AI to better understand their target audience, tailor products or services to specific needs, and strategically position their business for success.

Financial Planning and Projections

AI tools transform financial planning by providing accurate forecasts and budgeting assistance. These tools analyse historical data and current market conditions to offer realistic revenue, cost estimates, and cash flow analysis. This precision in financial planning ensures that moms will be able to make informed decisions about investments, pricing strategies, and managing business finances effectively.

Risk Management

Risk is inevitable in business, but AI can significantly aid in its assessment and mitigation. By analysing market trends and historical data, AI helps identify potential risks, including economic factors, industry-specific challenges, and regulatory changes. This foresight allows for developing robust contingency plans, ensuring the business remains resilient.

Operational Efficiency

AI's contribution to operational efficiency is profound. From automating routine tasks to optimising business processes, AI tools help streamline operations. This enhances productivity and affords moms more time to focus on strategic aspects of the business or attend to family needs. AI-driven project management tools assist in task scheduling, deadline management, and workflow optimisation, ensuring the smooth running of business operations.

Marketing and Customer Engagement

In marketing, AI's role is transformative. From personalised marketing strategies to customer relationship management, AI tools provide insights for targeted campaigns and effective communication. AI can analyse customer data to customise marketing messages, predict buying patterns, and improve customer engagement. This personalised approach in marketing leads to higher customer satisfaction and loyalty.

Adaptability and Continuous Learning

One of the most significant advantages of AI is its ability to adapt and learn continually. AI systems evolve with the changing market conditions, offering ongoing insights and recommendations. This adaptability ensures the business stays ahead of the curve, adjusting strategies in real-time for optimum performance.

For mompreneurs, AI in business planning and management isn't just about leveraging technology; it's about creating opportunities for growth while maintaining a harmonious balance between professional and personal life. AI empowers moms to build and manage successful businesses with efficiency, insight, and foresight, paving the way for sustainable growth and success. In embracing AI, mompreneurs are not just adopting new technology but opening doors to innovative ways of doing business in the digital age.

6.3. Digital Marketing and Customer Engagement with AI

Using AI in Digital Marketing and Customer Engagement

Artificial Intelligence (AI) has become a cornerstone in revolutionising digital marketing and customer engagement strategies in the digital age. The capability of AI to sift through extensive data sets, forecast customer actions, and tailor interactions renders it an indispensable tool for businesses seeking to improve their digital marketing strategies and more successfully engage with their customers. Here's a comprehensive look at how AI can be utilised in these areas:

Personalised Customer Experiences

AI excels in creating personalised experiences for customers. AI can tailor content, product recommendations, and marketing messages to individual users by analysing past behaviour, preferences, and interactions. This personalisation can occur on websites, email marketing campaigns, or even in targeted social media ads, ensuring customers see the most relevant content.

Chatbots and Virtual Assistants

AI-powered virtual assistants and chatbox can handle customer inquiries in real-time, providing instant support. These tools can answer common questions, guide users through purchases, and provide personalised recommendations, improving the customer service experience and freeing human resources for more complex tasks.

Predictive Analytics

AI's predictive capabilities are a game-changer in marketing. By analysing consumer data and market trends, AI can predict future buying behaviours and trends, allowing businesses to strategise and tailor their marketing efforts proactively. This can include determining the right time to launch a new product or allocating marketing budgets most effectively.

Content Generation and Optimisation

AI tools can help in content creation and optimisation. AI algorithms can generate essential content for articles, social media posts, and ad copy. Additionally, AI can optimise content for search engines (SEO), improving visibility and driving organic traffic.

Email Marketing Automation

AI enhances email marketing by segmenting mailing lists based on user behaviour and preferences, optimising email content for different segments, and identifying the optimal moments for sending emails to boost the rates of opening and clicking through.

Social Media Insights

AI can analyse social media data to gather insights into customer sentiment, brand perception, and trending topics. This can inform content strategy, brand positioning, and even product development.

Ad Targeting and Optimisation

In digital advertising, AI algorithms can optimise ad spending by targeting users more likely to convert and adjust bids in real-time. AI can also test different ad formats and placements to determine what works best for specific audiences.

Voice Search Optimisation

With the rise of voice assistants like Alexa and Google Assistant, optimising content for voice search is becoming increasingly important. AI can help businesses adapt their SEO strategy for voice queries, which are more conversational and longer than text-based searches.

Real-Time Analytics and Reporting

AI tools offer real-time analytics and reporting, providing businesses with up-to-date insights into the performance of their marketing campaigns. This enables quick adjustments and more dynamic marketing strategies.

In conclusion, AI's role in digital marketing and customer engagement is multifaceted and profoundly impactful. By leveraging the capabilities of AI, businesses can deliver more personalised experiences, engage customers more effectively, and optimise their marketing efforts for better results. As AI progresses, its functionalities will become increasingly refined, presenting greater possibilities for businesses to engage in meaningful connections with their customers. AI in digital marketing is no longer just an advantage; staying competitive in the rapidly changing digital landscape is becoming necessary.

6.4. Sales and Revenue Growth with AI

How AI Can Aid in Increasing Sales and Revenue

In today's highly competitive business landscape, Artificial Intelligence (AI) is a transformative force, particularly in boosting sales and revenue. Its integration into various business operations can lead to more efficient processes, better customer experiences, and enhanced profitability. Here's how AI can be a pivotal tool for businesses in their pursuit of increased sales and revenue:

Personalised Customer Experiences

AI excels in personalising customer interactions. By analysing customer data, AI can tailor product recommendations, marketing messages, and shopping experiences to individual preferences. This level of personalisation improves customer satisfaction and significantly increases the likelihood of sales.

Predictive Analytics for Targeted Marketing

AI's predictive analytics can forecast consumer behaviour and preferences, allowing businesses to target potential customers with the right products at the right time. Companies can craft targeted marketing campaigns by predicting what customers are more likely to buy, leading to higher conversion rates.

Optimised Pricing Strategies

AI algorithms can adjust prices based on demand, market conditions, and customer profiles. This dynamic pricing strategy ensures businesses maximise their revenue potential without alienating customers with overly high prices.

Enhanced Customer Service with Chatbots

AI-powered chatbots provide instant, 24/7 customer service. They can handle inquiries, provide product recommendations, and even assist in sales. This improves the customer experience and frees up human resources to focus on more complex sales tasks.

Streamlining the Sales Process

AI can streamline sales by automating tasks such as lead qualification and data entry. This increases the efficiency of sales teams, allowing them to focus on closing deals and building customer relationships.

E-commerce Optimisation

AI can optimise website layouts, search functionalities, and product placements for online retailers based on user behaviour and preferences. This creates a more intuitive and enjoyable shopping experience, encouraging more purchases.

Data-Driven Decision Making

AI's ability to analyse vast amounts of data provides businesses valuable insights. These insights inform strategic decisions regarding product development, marketing strategies, and customer engagement, which are vital for driving sales.

AI in Supply Chain Management

AI can enhance the efficiency of inventory management and streamline supply chain operations, ensuring items are in stock and readily available. This efficiency reduces the likelihood of lost sales due to inventory shortages and enhances overall customer satisfaction.

Social Media Insights for Marketing

AI tools can analyse social media trends and consumer sentiments, giving businesses insights into what products or services are trending. This allows businesses to change their marketing efforts to capitalise on these trends.

Real-Time Analytics for Agile Responses

AI provides real-time analytics, enabling businesses to quickly their strategies in response to market changes or customer feedback. This agility ensures that companies remain competitive and responsive to customer needs.

Incorporating AI into sales and marketing strategies is no longer just an option; it's necessary for businesses seeking growth and increased profitability. AI offers many ways to boost sales and revenue, from personalising customer experiences to optimising pricing and streamlining sales processes. As AI technology advances, its role in driving business success becomes increasingly significant. For businesses, leveraging AI is vital to staying ahead in a rapidly evolving marketplace and achieving sustained revenue growth.

6.5. Balancing Business and Motherhood

Balancing business and motherhood requires strategic planning and mindful prioritisation. Moms can achieve this equilibrium by setting clear boundaries between work and family time, ensuring each has a dedicated space. Effective time management is crucial; using digital calendars helps schedule and stick to work tasks, family activities, and personal time. Embracing technology for automating business processes and organising family responsibilities can significantly save time.

Delegating and outsourcing tasks at home and in business can alleviate the pressure of trying to do it all. Building a support network of family, friends, and professional contacts is invaluable for sharing responsibilities and gaining emotional support.

Equally important is self-care; maintaining personal well-being is essential to perform optimally in both roles. Flexibility and adaptability are key; understanding that some days will be more business-focused while others family-centred helps maintain a realistic approach to balancing both roles. Lastly, focusing on quality time with family, even if limited, ensures that moments spent together are meaningful and fulfilling, contributing to a well-rounded and satisfying balance between business aspirations and the joys of motherhood.

Starting and running a home-based business as a full-time mother is no small feat. AI can be a valuable ally in this journey, helping you identify opportunities, manage your business efficiently, and grow your customer base. The next chapter will explore how AI can aid in creative pursuits, enhancing your personal and professional fulfilment.

Chapter 7: AI for Creative Pursuits

Exploring Creativity with the Help of AI

In the modern digital age, Artificial Intelligence (AI) has become a powerful tool for enhancing and exploring creativity, especially for moms who might be juggling various responsibilities. AI technology offers innovative ways to engage in creative pursuits, making it easier to explore new hobbies or enhance existing skills. Here's how moms can harness AI to fuel their creativity:

AI in Art and Design: AI art tools like DeepArt and Prisma transform ordinary photos into artistic masterpieces by applying the styles of famous artists. For graphic design, platforms like Canva use AI to suggest layouts, colour schemes, and fonts, simplifying design tasks. Autodesk SketchBook and Adobe Photoshop offer AI features that assist in sketching and editing, making professional-grade design more accessible.

Creative Writing and Blogging: AI writing assistants, such as Grammarly or Hemingway Editor, help in refining written content, from correcting grammar to suggesting stylistic improvements. These tools can be invaluable for blogging, storytelling, or even professional writing.

Crafting and DIY Projects: AI-driven platforms suggest personalised crafting ideas and DIY projects based on past activities and current trends. They can provide inspiration and step-by-step guidance for a variety of creative projects.

Culinary Exploration: AI in cooking apps like Plant Jammer or IBM Chef Watson suggest recipes based on available ingredients, dietary preferences, or desired cuisines. This encourages culinary experimentation and simplifies meal planning.

Music and Audio Creation: AI music apps such as Amper Music or Google Magenta aid in composing music, generating tunes, or creating soundtracks for videos. These tools can be great for moms interested in exploring music production.

Learning and Skill Development: AI-powered educational platforms offer personalised learning experiences. Moms can explore online courses in areas like photography, painting, or digital arts, tailored to their skill level and interests.

Photography Enhancement: AI photo-editing tools, including Adobe Lightroom and Luminar, provide features like automated editing and style transfer, helping to enhance photos creatively with minimal effort.

Fashion and Personal Style: For fashion enthusiasts, AI in apps like Stitch Fix or Myntra offers personalised outfit recommendations, helping moms explore new styles and fashion trends.

Home Decoration and Gardening: AI apps assist in interior design and gardening, offering layout suggestions, colour coordination, and plant care advice, perfect for creative home improvement projects.

Mental and Emotional Creativity: AI apps like Woebot or Headspace use AI to provide mental wellness support through creative problem-solving, mindfulness practices, and cognitive behavioural techniques.

In conclusion, AI opens up a world of creative possibilities for moms. Whether it's through art and design, writing, crafting, cooking, or learning new skills, AI tools provide the resources and inspiration to explore and express creativity in various domains. These technologies not only make creative endeavours more accessible but also offer a flexible and efficient way to engage in creative activities amidst the busy schedule of motherhood. With AI, the journey of creativity can be both rewarding and enriching, allowing moms to discover new passions or deepen existing ones.

Chapter 8: Embracing AI for a Brighter Tomorrow

Achieving Harmony in a Tech-Enhanced World

As a full-time mother, balancing the myriad aspects of your life is crucial for your well-being and your family. I hope this book has helped you to explore how AI can help maintain this balance, enhancing productivity and ensuring you have time for what matters most.

Efficient time management is vital to a balanced life:

- AI-Powered Scheduling Tools: Discover AI tools that help you manage your calendar, set reminders for important tasks, and find the best appointment times.

- Task Automation: Learn how AI can automate routine tasks, from sorting emails to managing household chores, freeing up time for you and your family.

- Prioritisation Algorithms: Understand how AI can assist in prioritising your tasks based on urgency and importance, helping you focus on what truly matters.

Managing stress is vital for a healthy life:

- Mindfulness and Meditation Apps: Explore AI-driven apps that tailor mindfulness exercises and meditations to your stress level and preferences.

- Sleep Improvement Tools: Find out how AI can analyse your sleep patterns and recommend better sleep quality.

- AI-Assisted Fitness Routines: Learn about AI tools that suggest personalised fitness routines, helping you stay active and reduce stress.

While technology can be beneficial, setting boundaries is essential:

- Digital Well-being Tools: Discover tools that help you monitor and limit your technology usage, ensuring you maintain a healthy relationship with your devices.

- Family Tech-Time Management: Learn about apps that assist in managing the amount of time your family spends on devices, promoting more in-person interactions.

Continued learning is essential for personal growth:

- Customised Learning Platforms: Explore AI-driven platforms that suggest courses and learning paths tailored to your interests and career aspirations.

- Skill-Building Apps: Understand how AI can flexibly and efficiently help you build new skills, from languages to professional competencies.

Maintaining strong family relationships is crucial:

- AI in Family Activities and Planning: Discover AI tools that suggest family activities, vacations, and outings based on everyone's interests and schedules.

- Communication Enhancers: Learn about AI solutions that assist in managing family communications, scheduling quality time, and organising family events.

The Journey Continues

As we conclude our exploration of how AI can transform the lives of full-time mothers, it is essential to reflect on the journey we've taken together. From understanding the basics of AI to integrating it into various aspects of your daily life, this book has aimed to demystify AI and demonstrate its practical applications for enhancing your role as a mother, an entrepreneur, a creative, and a lifelong learner.

AI, as we've seen, is not just a futuristic concept; it's a present reality that offers tools and opportunities to make our lives more manageable, fulfilling, and enriched. By embracing AI, you can open doors to efficient household management, support your children's education, maintain health and wellness, manage finances, start and grow a home-based business, pursue creative passions, and maintain a balanced and joyful life.

Remember, the key to successfully integrating AI into your life is to view it as a complement to your human capabilities, not a replacement. It's about using AI to enhance your strengths, compensate for limitations, and give you more time and energy for what truly matters – your family, passions, and personal growth.

As "The Power of AI Mom" concludes, remember that your journey with AI is just beginning. The pages of this book are merely the first steps towards a future where AI and motherhood go hand in hand. Keep exploring, keep growing, and let AI guide you to a life of greater ease, opportunity, and fulfilment.

In closing, let this book remind you of your strength and capability as a mother and an individual. AI is a tool, but the true power lies within you – the power to adapt, learn, and thrive in an ever-changing world. The future is bright, and with AI as your ally, there's no limit to what you can achieve. The Power of AI Mom is not just about technology; it's about the strength, resilience, and love that defines motherhood. AI is here to illuminate your path as you navigate the remarkable journey of motherhood.

Appendices

Appendix A: Glossary of AI Terms

1. Artificial Intelligence (AI): A field within computer science focused on developing systems capable of executing tasks that typically require human intelligence. These tasks include learning, decision-making, problem-solving, perception, and language understanding.

2. Machine Learning: A division of AI that allows machines to autonomously learn and enhance their performance over time without requiring direct programming.

3. Algorithm: A collection of guidelines or directives provided to a computer, designed to assist it in executing a particular task or addressing problems.

4. Natural Language Processing (NLP): A field of AI that focuses on the interaction between computers and humans through natural language. The goal is for computers to process and understand human language.

5. Chatbot: A chatbot is a software application designed to simulate conversation with human users, especially over the internet. Chatbots are widely used for various purposes, such as customer service, information acquisition, and e-commerce, providing users with quick and automated responses to their inquiries.

6. Robotics: Robotics is a branch of engineering and science that involves the design, construction, operation, and use of robots. Robots can be programmed to perform various tasks autonomously or semi-autonomously. The field of robotics continually evolves as technological advancements, such as AI and machine learning, expand the capabilities and applications of robots in various industries and aspects of life.

7. Facial Recognition Technology: Facial recognition technology is biometric software that can identify or verify a person's identity using their face. It captures, analyses, and compares patterns based on the person's facial contours. The technology works by using a digital image or a video frame from a video source and then detecting and mapping facial features from the visual data. These features are then compared to a database of known faces to find matches.

8. Data Analytics: Examining data sets to draw conclusions about the information they contain. In AI, analytics often involve sophisticated data patterns and computational algorithms.

9. Smart Home Devices: Home appliances and devices that use internet connectivity and AI to enhance functionalities, such as learning user behaviours and automating tasks.

10. Cybersecurity: Cybersecurity in AI refers to the measures and practices employed to protect artificial intelligence systems from cyber threats and ensure their secure operation. As AI systems process vast amounts of data and often make autonomous decisions, they can be targets for cyberattacks that aim to manipulate, disrupt, or gain unauthorised access to these systems.

11. Internet of Things (IoT): The Internet of Things (IoT) refers to the network of physical objects ("things") that are embedded with sensors, software, and other technologies to connect and exchange data with other devices and systems over the internet. These objects range from ordinary household items like refrigerators and thermostats to sophisticated industrial tools.

12. Deep Learning: Deep learning is an advanced subset of machine learning, a type of artificial intelligence (AI) that mimics the workings of the human brain in processing data and creating patterns for decision-making.

13. Predictive Analytics: Predictive analytics is a branch of advanced analytics that uses historical data, statistical algorithms, and machine learning techniques to identify the likelihood of future outcomes. It involves analysing past and current data to predict future events or trends.

14. Telehealth: Telehealth refers to using digital information and communication technologies, like computers and mobile devices, to access healthcare services remotely and manage your healthcare.

15. Digital Footprint: The record of your interactions and activities online. It represents your online history and can be accessed or viewed by others, including companies, advertisers, and potential employers.

Appendix B: List of Resources

This appendix provides a curated list of resources, including websites, apps, and tools, which can further assist in exploring the concepts of AI as discussed in this book.

Websites for AI Education and News:

MIT Technology Review (AI Section)

- Stay informed about the latest in AI technology and research.

- technologyreview.com

AI Trends

- Insights and trends in AI for various industries and applications.

- aitrends.com

Towards Data Science

- Offers articles and tutorials on AI, machine learning, and data science.

- towardsdatascience.com

Educational Apps and Tools:

Duolingo

- Language learning app using AI for personalised lesson plans.

- duolingo.com

Khan Academy

- Offers a variety of educational resources for all ages, with some AI-driven courses.

- khanacademy.org

Photomath

- AI-based app that helps solve mathematical problems with step-by-step explanations.

- photomath.com

Fitness and Health:

MyFitnessPal

- Tracks diet and exercise, using AI to personalise diet plans.
- myfitnesspal.com

Fitbit

- Wearables that track health data, with AI-powered insights.
- fitbit.com

Headspace

- Offers AI-driven personalised meditation and mindfulness practices.
- headspace.com

Productivity Tools:

Trello

- Project management tool that can be used for organising household tasks and schedules.
- trello.com

Google Calendar

- AI-powered scheduling and time management tool.
- calendar.google.com

RescueTime

- AI-driven productivity tracking tool, useful for managing time effectively.
- rescuetime.com

Online Safety:

FamilyTime

- Parental control app for monitoring and managing children's digital usage.

- familytime.io

Net Nanny

- Provides safe internet browsing for children with AI-driven content screening.
- netnanny.com

AI Learning for Kids:

Scratch

- Introduces children to the basics of coding, with an AI component for advanced learners.
- scratch.mit.edu

Tynker

- Coding for kids, with AI-based learning paths.
- tynker.com

These resources are intended to provide parents and children alike with tools and information to better understand and utilise AI in various aspects of their lives, from education and health to productivity and online safety.

Appendix C: Practical Exercises and Tips

This appendix offers practical exercises and tips to reinforce the concepts discussed in "The Power of AI Mom: A Beginner's Guide to Utilising AI for Productive Parenting." These activities are designed to help mothers integrate AI effectively into their daily lives, covering aspects of household management, personal development, children's education, and more.

1. Household Management with AI:

- Exercise: Set up a smart home device (like a smart thermostat or voice assistant) and create a weekly routine that includes automated reminders for household tasks.
- Tip: Use voice commands to add tasks and shopping items to your digital list as you think of them, keeping your hands free for other activities.

2. Personal Development through AI Learning Platforms:

- Exercise: Enrol in an online course on an AI-driven learning platform. Set a goal to complete a module each week.

- Tip: Choose a course that aligns with your interests or goals for personal or professional development.

3. Enhancing Children's Education with AI:

- Exercise: Introduce your child to an AI-based educational app tailored to their age and interests. Schedule regular, but limited, sessions.

- Tip: Engage with your child post-session to discuss what they learned, reinforcing the material.

4. Fitness Routine Using AI Apps:

- Exercise: Use a fitness app with AI personalisation to create a 4-week workout plan. Track your progress within the app.

- Tip: Set realistic fitness goals and use the app's reminders to stay consistent.

5. Meal Planning with AI:

- Exercise: Use an AI-powered recipe app to plan your meals for the week based on dietary preferences and ingredients in your pantry.

- Tip: Involve the family in meal planning, making it a fun and collaborative activity.

6. Budgeting with AI Tools:

- Exercise: Implement an AI-driven budgeting tool. Regularly monitor your spending and adjust budgets based on the tool's insights.

- Tip: Use the insights from the app to identify spending trends and areas for savings.

7. Mindfulness and Mental Well-being:

- Exercise: Practice mindfulness using an AI-based meditation app. Dedicate a few minutes daily for guided sessions.

- Tip: Choose different types of meditation within the app to find what works best for you.

8. Smart Shopping with AI:

- Exercise: Install a price comparison or deal-finding app for your online shopping needs. Use it for a month to find the best deals.

- Tip: Use the app's alert feature to get notified about price drops on products you need.

9. Learning and Discussing AI Ethics with Children:

- Exercise: Have a family discussion about the ethical use of AI, using examples from media or daily life.

- Tip: Use storytelling to illustrate points about privacy, data sharing, and digital footprint.

10. Starting a Home-Based Business with AI Tools:

- Exercise: Explore AI tools for market research and business planning. Start by drafting a simple business plan using these tools.

- Tip: Utilise AI-driven social media management tools to plan and automate your business's online presence.

These exercises and tips are intended to provide hands-on experience and practical knowledge, helping to seamlessly incorporate AI into various aspects of daily life, enhancing efficiency, learning, and overall well-being.